W9-CGK-872

Practical Time Management

HOW TO MAKE THE MOST OF YOUR MOST PERISHABLE RESOURCE

Marion E. Haynes

CRISP PUBLICATIONS, INC.
Menlo Park, California

Copyright © 1991
by Crisp Publications, Inc.
1200 Hamilton Court
Menlo Park, California 94025
original copyright © 1985
by PennWell Publishing Co.

Library of Congress cataloging in publication data

Haynes, Marion E.
    Practical time management.

    1. Time management.   I. Title.

HD38.H393   1984   640'.43   84-20742
ISBN 1-56052-018-3

Printed in the United States of America
i

This book is printed
on recyclable paper
with soy ink.

This book is dedicated to Curtis, Sharman, and Sara, with the hope that they learn to use their time wisely.

Contents

Preface

Do you feel pressured by too much to do and too little time in which to do it? Or do you simply want to get more things done? Both of these situations suggest a need for better time management.

Time, like any other resource, can be managed by a set of principles and a variety of techniques. This study guide will lead you through an analysis of your time management problems and present to you the principles and techniques you need to become master of your time rather than a slave to it. The guide is divided into eight sections covering the following topics:

- Introduction to time management concepts
- Analyzing your job responsibilities
- Analyzing how you use your time
- How to make full use of your staff
- How to plan effectively
- How to cope with common time wasters
- Developing your action plan
- Following up to stay on track

This study guide will help you become a better manager of your time. However, it won't manage your time for you. That is left to you. Effective time management is basically an experience in self-discipline. You are the key to success. If you complete this guide—it will take you about eight weeks—and use the principles and techniques presented, you will get more done and will enjoy doing it.

Practical Time Management

Time Management Concepts

OBJECTIVES

- **Consider your present use of time.**
- **Highlight the benefits of using your time effectively.**
- **Determine the portion of your schedule over which you have control.**
- **Introduce the principles of analysis and planning.**

Everyone has 24 hours each day—no more, no less. Yet very few people feel they have just enough time. There's nothing you can do to change the *amount* of time available to you. You can only choose how you will *use* it.

Some people feel they have too much time. They are bored and disheartened. They don't know what to do to gain personal satisfaction from the time available to them. They simply sit and let it tick away—one second at a time.

Others feel they have too little time. They are hurried, stressed, frustrated. They feel there are too many demands placed upon them. They never have time to give a job the attention it deserves—they never have time to plan. These people don't know what to do to gain control of the use of their time. They scurry around trying to do everything and are dissatisfied when they can't get it all done at the quality level they would prefer.

Where are you? (Circle one of the numbers below.)

Too Much	5	4	3	2	1	0	1	2	3	4	5	Too Little
Time						Just Right						Time

You probably feel you have too little time. Right? But consider a couple of points. If you had 2 extra hours each day (a) what would you do with the time and (b) how long would it be until that time was taken up the same way your present time is so that you wouldn't be any better off? Answer the following by putting an X in front of each that applies:

If I had 2 extra hours a day I would:

_____ 1. Do more planning.

_____ 2. Do more reading.

_____ 3. Spend more time talking to members of my work group.

_____ 4. Put in less hours at the office each day.

_____ 5. Develop new areas of opportunity or better ways of handling my present responsibilities.

_____ 6. _____

_____

Benefits of Better Time Utilization

These longer-term activities, which are the basic foundation of future survival, are often set aside in order to respond to immediate demands. Consider the following:

- *Planning.* Setting a future course for your area of responsibility and laying out a plan to achieve it results in worthwhile contribution. It helps move you from a reactive mode to a proactive one. It puts you in charge of your own destiny.
- *Reading.* Keeping up to date in your field is mandatory with the current rate of growth in information. What new technologies are developing? Where is your field of knowledge headed? These questions are answered by selectively reading the journals of your trade or profession.
- *Talking.* The cooperative effort of others is required to attain your objectives. Talking is the vehicle for building and maintaining relationships, which ensures cooperation when it is needed.
- *Relaxing.* You can only do so much. When you do not take appropriate time to relax and recover from the demands of your job, your health will suffer.
- *Thinking.* Improved methods and new opportunities come about as a result of innovation. That takes time to think through and develop as well as time to gain support and approval for changes.

Who Controls Your Schedule?

To begin to engage in these longer-term activities, you must make room for them on your daily schedule. This frequently is a function of the extent to which you believe you have control over how you use your time.

Where are you? (Circle one of the numbers below.)

| I Have Total Control | 10 | 9 | 8 | 7 | 6 | 5 | 4 | 3 | 2 | 1 | 0 | I Have No Control |

Hardly anyone has total control over his or her schedule. There will always be someone, or something, making demands. However, nearly everyone has some control, and probably you have more control than you realize.

Summary and Conclusions

Time is a unique resource. Everyone has the same amount. It cannot be accumulated. You can't turn it on or off. It can't be replaced. It has to be spent at the rate of sixty seconds every minute.

Time management, like other management problems, is subject to the principles of analysis and planning. To apply these principles, you must know how you use your time, problems you encounter in using your time wisely, and what causes them. From this data base you can plan and control your use of time to improve both your effectiveness and efficiency.

Time management is a personal process. Any system must be adapted to your personal style and the situation within which you operate. It takes strong personal commitment to change old habits. However, the choice is available, and it is yours for the taking. If you choose, you can begin to reap greater returns from your time investment. This study guide will point the way. It is up to you to do something with it.

OBJECTIVES

The objectives of this study guide are to:
- **Help you determine how you presently use your time.**
- **Help you determine the portion of your time over which you have control.**
- **Help you make the most effective use of that portion of your time under your control.**
- **Help you handle the remainder of your time in the most efficient way.**

IN RETROSPECT

Look back over the ideas presented in this section and think about them in the context of your present job and work environment.

1. What aspects of your job do you seem to have least control over?

　_____

　_____

　_____

　_____

　_____

2. What tasks, or activities, are you engaged in that take a lot of time, yet don't seem to make much of a contribution to your own or your work group's objectives?

   a. _____

   b. _____

   c. _____

   d. _____

   e. _____

   f. _____

   g. _____

   h. _____

   i. _____

3. Are you really interested in improving your time utilization? Why or why not? What would be the benefits? What are the potential costs? Complete Exercise 1−1 to help you with this assessment.

　_____

　_____

　_____

　_____

　_____

EXERCISE 1–1. How You Use the 168 Hours in Your Week

	Usually	Occasionally	Seldom
1. Do you spend your time the way you really want to?	———	———	———
2. Do you feel harried, obligated to do too many things you really don't want to do?	———	———	———
3. Do you get a feeling of self-satisfaction and accomplishment from your work?	———	———	———
4. Do you work long hours? How many? _____ hours.	———	———	———
5. Do you take work home evenings or weekends?	———	———	———
6. Is there stress in your work? Do you feel tense and insecure?	———	———	———
7. Do you have guilt feelings about not doing a better job?	———	———	———
8. Is your job fun?	———	———	———
9. Do you feel in control of the use of your time?	———	———	———
10. Can you find large blocks of uninterrupted time when you need to?	———	———	———
11. Do you have time to keep physically fit?	———	———	———
12. Do you have time to take the vacations and long weekends you would like?	———	———	———
13. Do you put off doing the difficult, boring, or unpleasant parts of your job?	———	———	———
14. Do you feel you must always be busy doing something productive?	———	———	———
15. Do you feel guilty when you goof off for a while?	———	———	———

From *Successful Time Management,* Jack D. Ferner, pp. 6-7, New York, NY: John Wiley & Sons, © 1980. Used by permission of the publisher. All rights reserved.

Your Job—What You Are Responsible for Accomplishing

OBJECTIVES

- Determine the scope of your job responsibilities.
- Develop a focus on high-priority responsibilities.
- Reconcile any differences between your perception and your supervisor's perception of your responsibilities and priorities.
- Examine the potential contribution of objectives to your area of responsibility.

A job can be viewed from three different perspectives (see Figure 2–1). One view is your perception of what the job is like—what you see as your duties and responsibilities and the relative importance of each of them. Another view is how the job ideally ought to be. That is, if you had total control to organize it any way you wanted, what would it look like? Finally, a job can be viewed from the perspective of how it actually is. Regardless of how you perceive it, regardless of how it ought to be, this is the way it is experienced by you. Consider Figure 2–1. Your optimistic goal should be to bring these three circles together so they appear as one.

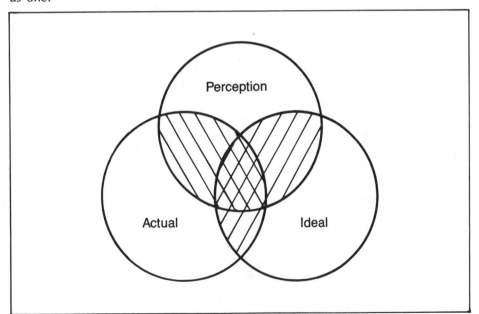

FIGURE 2–1.   Three different views of your job

Your Job Responsibilities

What does your supervisor or manager expect you to get done? Toward what ends should your efforts be directed? Only by examining these issues can you begin to gain insight into your job and your time problems. With the insight gained you will be able to make some decisions about what changes should be made in reallocating your time for better results.

Most people have never attempted to analyze their job in this manner. You may find it difficult in your first attempt. But stay with it until you're satisfied with your results. It will be worth the effort. Break down whatever you're doing into as many categories as necessary for the exercise to make sense to you. Don't get hung up on questions of technique or form. Even an imperfect product will contribute to your understanding. On the other hand, be sure to use enough categories so that someone else can understand the nature and purpose of your job.

Start your analysis by considering where you are expected to invest time, energy, talent, and other company resources. This will include both output you personally generate as well as that which is generated by others as a result of your planning, coordinating, directing, and organizing activities. Start with the normal or routine output for which you are responsible but don't neglect the problem-solving and anticipation/innovation responsibilities you have.

Setting priorities on your job responsibilities draws on your experience and judgment. You should view your personal assignments of priorities as a starting point from which you and your supervisor will negotiate an understanding. Consider the consequences of doing or not doing each item on your list. The item with the most significant consequences to the company or your department should be your number one priority item.

In completing your analysis, watch out for the activities trap. There usually is a substantial difference between an activity and a responsibility. For example, "attend team meetings" is an activity. "Communicate with team members" and "participate in team decisions" may more closely approximate your responsibilities. You obviously can make a case that "communicate" and "participate" are activities, also. The distinction hinges on the question, "Why do I do that?" You carry out activities to fulfill responsibilities.

Complete the Job Responsibility Analysis forms in Exercises 2–1 and 2–2.

Setting Objectives

Setting objectives can add clarity, focus, and purpose to most jobs. Without objectives, planning is usually done immediately prior to or along with action. Frequent changes in plans are often experienced, usually as a result of either a lack of time to consider all alternatives or a lack of a predetermined outcome to be achieved. This approach is often referred to as firefighting or operating by the seat of the pants. It is illustrated by the person who comes to work with no clear idea of the day's activities. Things begin to happen—the mail arrives, the phone rings, people

EXERCISE 2–1.   Job Responsibility Analysis Worksheet

Instructions: List your job responsibilities as they occur to you. After each one is listed, assign it a priority with *A* being high, *B* moderate, and *C* low. Then, rate the level of enjoyment you experience in carrying out this responsibility on a 1 to 5 scale with 5 being high.

Responsibility	Priority	Enjoyment

Note: Best results are usually achieved by making a first attempt then setting it aside for a couple of days before finalizing.

EXERCISE 2–2. Job Responsibility Analysis

Instructions: Edit the listing on your worksheet and transfer it to this form in priority order. Now, estimate the percentage of your time devoted to each responsibility and record what you consider to be an ideal percentage.

Responsibility	Priority	Enjoyment	Time Distribution		
			Est.	Ideal	Actual*

*Complete this column after analyzing the time log in Section 3.

stop by. The individual reacts and responds to these various demands. A flurry of activity with considerable effort is put forth, but often few results are achieved.

When objectives exist, the results to be achieved are defined in advance and the action steps necessary to achieve those results are specified. Thus, upon reporting to work on any given day, an individual knows what must be done to stay on course in pursuit of the desired outcome.

Opportunities for Setting Objectives. Your total effort typically cannot be directed toward some predetermined objective. There will be unexpected demands that require a response. Time must be set aside to address those demands. Two thoughts are worth considering. Both require some reflection on the nature of these demands you have experienced over the past several months. If, upon reflection, you note a recurring pattern of events, you can anticipate that this experience will continue. You should be ready to handle it when it occurs. If no pattern is noted, simply dedicate a portion of your time to deal with the unanticipated demands that you know are going to occur.

Another perspective on setting objectives can be gained from considering your job in terms of an input/output analysis. Consider Figure 2–2.

This figure suggests that things on which about 80% of one's time and effort are spent produce only about 20% of that individual's results—thus, the label "trivial many." On the other hand, those things commanding the other 20% of one's time and effort produce as much as 80% of one's overall results—thus, the

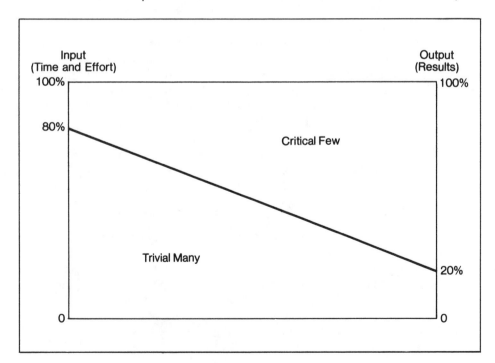

FIGURE 2–2. Input/output analysis

label "critical few." The purpose of objectives is to focus adequate attention on these critical few opportunities. Otherwise, there is a severe hazard that the trivial, time-consuming activities of the day will push the critical few entirely off the calendar (see Exhibit 2–1).

The critical few area contains two general categories of opportunity. One is innovation, that is, what new and different things could you do to improve the overall effectiveness of your unit or job. The other is problem-solving; that is, what impediments could you eliminate from the current situation to allow the normal flow of work to move more smoothly. These two categories become the prime candidates for objectives setting.

Writing Objectives. Statements of objectives should specify what is to be done by when. Cost limitations should be included as appropriate. The statement should definitely not include any reference to the means of accomplishing the objective. This only limits the range of opportunity available when the action-planning step is handled. These guidelines should be followed (see examples that follow):

- *Specific.*   The statement should say exactly what is to be achieved and to what extent. For example, to increase sales by 15%, to reduce absenteeism by 3 employee days per month, or to remodel warehouse according to approved plans and budgets.
- *Measurable.*   By being specific, objectives will be measurable. You will therefore know whether you have been successful at the end of the performance period.
- *Action-oriented.*   Objective statements should say what you are going to do. By being action-oriented they are more easily measured. You will know whether or not you did as you intended by the end of the period.
- *Realistic.*   Good objective statements are realistic. They might be optimistic at the outset; but as the means to achieve them are developed, they should move into the realm of realism. Avoid extremes—such as 100% or 0—that stand no chance of being accomplished.
- *Time-limited.*   Good objective statements have a time limit built into them by which time the results will be achieved. People respond to deadlines. Without them things can easily be pushed farther into the future.

Examples of Objective Statements

- Reduce respond time to customer inquiries from current average of 7 days to 4 days or less by end of third quarter.
- Increase participant to class size ratio to 0.96 or better by end of year.
- Complete the consolidation of the Birmingham, Atlanta, and Jacksonville districts within approved budget by end of second quarter.
- Recruit and orient two new process engineers by end of first quarter at a cost not to exceed $10,000 and 30 hours of my time.
- Eliminate filing backlog by end of February.

EXHIBIT 2–1. Tyranny of the Urgent

Have you ever wished for a thirty-hour day? Surely this extra time would relieve the tremendous pressure under which we live. Our lives leave a trail of unfinished tasks. Unanswered letters, unvisited friends, unwritten articles, and unread books haunt quiet moments when we stop to evaluate. We desperately need relief.

But would a thirty-hour day really solve the problem? Wouldn't we soon be just as frustrated as we are now with our twenty-four allotment? A mother's work is never finished, and neither is that of any manager, student, teacher, minister, or anyone else we know. Nor will the passage of time help us catch up. Children grow in number and age to require more of our time. Greater experience brings more exacting assignments. So we find ourselves working more and enjoying it less.

When we stop to evaluate, we realize that our dilemma goes deeper than shortage of time; it is basically the problem of priorities. Hard work does not hurt us. We all know what it is to go full speed for long hours, totally involved in an important task. The resulting weariness is matched by a sense of achievement and joy. Not hard work, but doubt and misgiving produce anxiety as we review a month or year and become oppressed by the pile of unfinished tasks. We sense demands have driven us onto a reef of frustration. We confess, quite apart from our sins, "we have left undone those things which we ought to have done; and we have done those things which we ought not to have done."

Several years ago an experienced cotton-mill manager said to me, "Your greatest danger is letting the urgent things crowd out the important." He didn't realize how hard his maxim hit. It often returns to haunt and rebuke me by raising the critical problem of priorities.

We live in constant tension between the urgent and the important. The problem is that the important task rarely must be done today, or even this week. The urgent task calls for instant action—endless demands, pressure every hour and day.

A man's home is no longer his castle; it is no longer a place away from urgent tasks because the telephone breaches the walls with imperious demands. The momentary appeal of these tasks seems irresistible and important, and they devour our energy. But in the light of time's perspective their deceptive prominence fades; with a sense of loss we recall the important tasks pushed aside. We realize we've become slaves to the "tyranny of the urgent."

Now that you know the principles involved in writing good objectives, complete Exercise 2–3. Remember, look for opportunities for improvement or problems to be solved.

Setting Priorities

When opportunities exceed resources, you must decide what is more important or what you would rather do. Nowhere is this more apparent than in the use of time. Rather than working more hours, the decision of what to do and what not to do must be made.

Setting priorities on the use of your time is a two-step process: (1) Make a list of opportunities or things to do and (2) prioritize the items on the list.

Use the ABC method to determine your priorities. This requires you to place each item on your list into one of the following three categories:

- *Priority A—Got-to-do's.*   These are the critical few items of highest value on your list. Some of the reasons an item may fall in this category include demands by higher management or important customers, significant deadlines, and potential contribution to business results.
- *Priority B—Ought-to-do's.*   These are the items of medium value. This category may include items that will contribute significantly to performance improvement but are not essential and items that have not yet become critical deadline problems.
- *Priority C—Nice-to-do's.*   This is the low-value category. While these are desirable items to get done, they could be eliminated, postponed, or scheduled during slack periods.

When you get your list prioritized, those items marked A should be the ones that yield the most value. You will get the most out of your time by doing them first and saving the B's and C's until later. If you like, you can further refine your list by prioritizing within your ABC categories. This will produce a list of A–1, A–2, A–3. . . B–1, B–2, B–3. . . C–1, C–2, C–3. . . .

The A's, B's, and C's are relative depending on your point of view. For example, a task might be an A priority while you are thinking of all the rewards that will come with its completion. But partway through, when the going gets tough, you drop it to a C priority. Was it an A or not? That is up to you. You are the best judge of your own priorities; if you are not satisfied with the way things come out, you need to improve your ability to focus on what is really important.

The A's, B's, and C's are also relative depending on what is on your list and when you prepare it. The A's generally stand out clearly in contrast to the less important B's and C's, and priorities may change over time. Today's B may become tomorrow's A as an important deadline approaches. Likewise, today's A may become tomorrow's C if it did not get done today and circumstances change.

A's, B's, and C's may also vary depending on the amount of time you choose to invest in a particular project. For example, you could probably satisfy your

EXERCISE 2–3. Writing Objectives for Your Job

In the following space, write five objective statements for your present job. What results would you like to achieve that would make a substantial contribution to your section or department? Remember—be sure the statements are specific, measurable, action-oriented, realistic, and time bound. Also, *do not* include any reference to how you plan to achieve the results specified.

1. _____

   _____

   _____

   _____

   _____

2. _____

   _____

   _____

   _____

   _____

3. _____

   _____

   _____

   _____

   _____

4. _____

   _____

   _____

   _____

   _____

5. _____

   _____

   _____

   _____

   _____

manager with about two hours of work on a report he wants. You feel it is a B, but you could really impress him with about four hours' effort. So you decide to make it an A and invest the four hours.

Obviously, it is not worthwhile to make a big effort for a task of little value. On the other hand, a project of high value can be worth a great deal of effort. Good prioritizing and planning let you reap maximum benefits from minimum time investments.

There's always time to do what's really important.

The problem is knowing what's important.

FIGURE 2–3. The key problem

Summary and Conclusions

The starting place, to begin to examine your use of time, is to understand your job responsibilities. This process reconciles your perception of your job with how it ought to be and how it actually is.

One key point from this analysis is the simple observation that you are now using all of your time. Therefore, you have to subtract something before you can add something else. If you want to spend more time in one responsibility area, you will have to reduce the time you are now spending in some other area.

One way to approach this subtracting and adding process is to rely on the priorities assigned to your job responsibilities. You may find it necessary to cut back the time spent on lower (C) priority responsibilities in order to free up adequate time to address higher (A) priority responsibilities.

Objectives setting is another way to impact your time allocation. The process of setting objectives is both a directive and motivating force. This force is further enhanced when you make a commitment to someone else to achieve the stated objectives. If you do not have objectives—no place at which you want to arrive—it doesn't really matter what you do or how you spend your time. But, when you have objectives to which you are willing to commit yourself, your activities take on meaning and purpose. And it becomes easier to choose between conflicting demands on your time.

IN RETROSPECT

Look back over the ideas presented in this section and think about them in the context of your present job and work environment.

1. To what extent has completing the Job Responsibility Analysis helped clarify the scope of your job? Comment on your observations regarding the perceived and ideal views of your job.

_____

_____

_____

_____

_____

_____

_____

_____

2. Compare the priority and enjoyment ratings assigned to each responsibility area. What cautions can you identify to avoid doing what you enjoy doing rather than what needs to be done?

_____

_____

_____

_____

_____

_____

_____

_____

3. Compare your estimate of time to the ideal time for each responsibility area. What opportunities do you see to subtract time from one area in order to add it to another? Caution: Don't make any changes until you have actual time data available.

_____

_____

_____

_____

_____

_____

_____

4. Reflect on the ideas presented in the text. What can you use? Do you currently set objectives for your job? If not, what potential does this idea hold for you? What other observations do you have after completing your Job Responsibility Analysis?

_____

_____

_____

_____

_____

_____

_____

5. When you are comfortable with your individual work, make an appointment with your supervisor and review your job responsibilities, priorities, time distribution, and objectives. To help prepare for this meeting, complete Exercises 2–4 and 2–5. After the discussion, what was your reaction to the experience? How do you feel about it?

_____

_____

_____

_____

_____

_____

EXERCISE 2–4. Relationship with Manager

Your response to the following 15 questions will help you evaluate your effectiveness. For each question circle the score that applies to you. Then total your score and rate yourself at the end of the exercise.

	Often	Sometimes	Rarely
1. Does your manager surprise you with rush jobs that could be more effectively accomplished by advance planning?	− 1	1	2
2. Do you interrupt the work of your manager in ways that could be avoided?	− 1	1	2
3. Do you feel there is training or additional experience you need to help you function more effectively in your present job?	− 1	1	2
4. Do you feel excessively dependent upon your manager in order to get your work done?	− 1	0	2
5. Does your manager often waste your time by being late for appointments or meetings?	− 1	0	2
6. Do you inform your manager whenever he (she) does something you would like him (her) to continue?	2	1	− 1
7. Does your manager give instructions to you as well as he (she) should?	2	1	− 1
8. Does your manager tend to oversupervise or overcontrol you and/or your staff?	− 1	0	2
9. Does your manager tend to generate unnecessary work for himself (herself) and/or for you?	− 1	0	2
10. Do you feel uncomfortable with your manager when discussing the priorities of work assignments?	− 1	0	2

EXERCISE 2–4.   *Continued*

	Often	Sometimes	Rarely
11. Does your manager bypass you by going directly to your staff regarding work activities?	−1	0	2
12. Does your manager switch work priorities on you?	−1	1	2
13. Does your manager permit and encourage you to act in his (her) behalf?	2	1	−1
14. Does your manager overdelegate to some staff members (your peers) and underdelegate to others?	−1	0	2
15. Does your manager keep you adequately informed of organizational matters that affect you and your operations?	2	1	−1
Column totals	——	——	——

Total score (all three columns): ____

Scores can range between 30 and −15. A score below 15 suggests that some changes are needed in your relationship with your manager.

EXERCISE 2-5. Relationships with Staff

Your response to the following 15 questions will help you evaluate your effectiveness. For each question circle the score that applies to you. Then total your score and rate yourself at the end of the exercise.

	Often	Sometimes	Rarely
1. Do you tend to generate unnecessary work for yourself and/or your staff?	−1	0	2
2. Are you readily accessible to your staff when they need you?	2	0	−1
3. Does your staff tend to upward-delegate problems to you?	−1	0	2
4. Do you encourage your staff to keep a daily "to do" list?	2	0	−1
5. Do you give instructions to your staff as well as you should?	2	1	−1
6. Do you waste the time of your staff by making them wait for you?	−1	0	2
7. Do you discuss team time problems with your staff?	2	1	−1
8. Do you invest time in training your staff?	2	1	−1
9. Do you tend to oversupervise or over-control your staff?	−1	0	2
10. Do you interrupt the work of your staff in ways that could be prevented?	−1	0	2
11. Do you reward your staff whenever they do something you would like continued?	2	0	−1
12. Do you feel the need to redo work done by your staff?	−1	0	2
13. Do you overdelegate to some staff members and underdelegate to others?	−1	0	2

EXERCISE 2–5. *Continued*

	Often	Sometimes	Rarely
14. Do you permit and encourage your staff to attend meetings in your behalf?	2	1	−1
15. Does each member of your staff understand the group objectives and his/her specific part?	2	0	−1
Column totals	___	___	___
Total score (all three columns): ___			

Scores can range between 30 and −15. A score below 15 suggests that some changes are needed in your relationships with your staff.

How You Use Your Time

OBJECTIVES

- **Determine how you spend your time.**
- **Determine any unnecessary or inappropriate activities that are consuming significant amounts of time.**
- **Identify opportunities for better time utilization.**

The starting point for making better use of your time is to find out how you are currently using it.

There is no question that most people are busy. It's a phenomenon of human nature. Most people would rather be busy doing something than be idle and bored. For example, think of a time when you couldn't do anything. Maybe you were ill, injured, or isolated for whatever reason. How long did it take you to become bored? Were you able to come up with some creative ways to occupy your time?

So it is in the workplace. If you don't have enough work to occupy your time, you become bored and begin to seek out creative ways to stay busy.

Gathering Data—The Time Log

The important first step in learning to make better use of your time is to gather reliable data.

You may well believe you know how you spend your day, but you probably don't. Countless studies have shown that most people can't even remember what they did yesterday with any substantial degree of accuracy! It's important to know how you currently spend your time. You can't determine how to improve unless you have reliable information. The way most people spend their time is a matter of habit and routine. You can change habits when you know what they are.

A time log is provided at the end of this section (Exercise 3–1). Pick out what appears to be a fairly typical week and keep track of all your time and what you are doing with it. Be very honest with yourself. Make entries in your time log at least twice a day—before lunch and before going home. This will prevent your forgetting the details and significance of activities.

The results of your Time Log will probably amaze you. You may discover that you actually use your time in different ways than you imagined.

Analyzing the Data

Consider a hypothetical situation. You receive a telephone call from the vice president of your organization. He asks whether you'd be interested in taking on a special assignment for which you are uniquely qualified. In this assignment you would report directly to him, and you would be involved in making some important decisions on issues critical to the company's future success. The assignment would involve some travel to places that you would enjoy visiting. Not only would the assignment provide an opportunity for you to make a significant contribution but also would provide career growth opportunities. While the duration of the assignment is indefinite at this time, it is estimated to take several months to complete.

The offer has only one catch. Because the assignment is part-time, involving an average of one day a week, you would not be relieved of any of your present duties and responsibilities. You would have to continue getting your present job done in the remaining four days. Would you take the assignment?

Ninety-nine percent of the people facing this opportunity would take the assignment. By doing so, they are saying that, if the motivation were powerful enough, they could either eliminate or do in much less time certain of their current duties without any significant negative consequences.

The reason that most people are able to find slack time, when sufficiently motivated to do so, is because of a prevalent norm of busyness. Not only do people like to keep busy, but it's expected of them by many managers and supervisors. Busyness becomes contagious as it is reinforced within the culture of work groups. It takes several people working together in an unconscious conspiracy to perpetuate too many time-wasting meetings, too much paper, too many reports of useless information, too cumbersome administrative procedures, too complicated an organization structure, too many studies, and too little action. Once these activities become part of a culture, they can be self-perpetuating.

Some busyness is brought about by the anxiety or uneasiness associated with certain job responsibilities. When an individual lacks the skills or confidence to handle an area of responsibility or when he considers the responsibility boring or meaningless, he tends to escape into time-wasting activities. A sufficient excuse then exists to justify not doing the undesirable. Unfortunately, as one gets caught up in unproductive activities, the responsibility being avoided tends to grow in significance, creating even greater anxiety, pressure, and frustration.

As you look over your completed time log, be particularly critical. Approach it as though you were trying to free up an extra day a week in order to be able to take on that special project. Three analyses will be helpful: necessity, appropriateness, and efficiency.

Test Necessity.   In the first analysis scrutinize each task or activity to make sure it is necessary—not just *nice*, but *necessary*. It is very common to continue doing things beyond their usefulness. For example, reports are summarized each month although the data are no longer used by anyone. It is also common to duplicate the work of someone else because of lack of trust in the other person's ability or interest in doing it properly. This analysis should reduce your job to its essential elements.

Test Appropriateness. When the essential tasks have been identified, the next analysis should determine who should appropriately perform them. This analysis should include an examination of appropriateness in terms of departmental or sectional alignment and appropriateness in terms of skills levels and authorities. In regard to the former, you may find tasks or activities that should be turned over to administrative support sections, such as finance, purchasing, or employee relations, or to technical support sections, such as engineering, inspection, or safety. In regard to the latter, you may find that you are doing work substantially beneath your skills level, which can be reassigned within your section.

Test Efficiency. This final analysis looks at the work remaining. When you are satisfied that you are doing necessary work that only you can do, you should ask the question: Is there a better way? This question encourages at least two avenues of pursuit. First, is there a faster, better way to get the job done by using updated technology? With current advances in data handling, storage, and retrieval, opportunities often exist to save considerable personal time. Second, can administrative procedures be established to handle recurring activities? This should include a consideration of developing worksheets and forms to simplify gathering, handling, and reporting information. Also, this analysis may pinpoint opportunities for better organization and planning, which will contribute to a more efficient use of your time.

There are only three ways to make better use of your time:

1. Discontinue low-priority tasks or activities

2. Get someone else to do a part of what you are now doing

3. Be more efficient in using your time

FIGURE 3–1. Choices available

Summary and Conclusions

An examination of how you are presently using your time is the first step in gaining more control of it. You must have specific, reliable information before you can analyze your present pattern of activities to determine opportunities for improvement.

Given reliable information, you can examine it from three points of view—necessity, appropriateness, and efficiency. These analyses normally reveal opportunities to discontinue certain tasks, pass others on to different people, and increase efficiency through technology, administrative procedures, and personal work habits. When subjected to such an analysis, nearly everyone's weekly schedule will yield 8 to 10 hours that can be better spent on more important activities.

EXERCISE 3–1. Instructions for Keeping Daily Time Log

- Select a fairly typical week. Avoid any with a holiday, vacation, sick leave, personal leave, etc.

- Record all activities at least every half hour. Be as specific as possible; for example, identify visitors and callers and record duration and topics of conversations. Be honest. Only you will have access to this information.

- Comment on each activity with a view to better time utilization. Did something take longer than usual? Why? Were you interrupted?

- At the end of the day indicate whether this day was typical, busier than usual, or less busy than usual. Comment as to why you believe the day was either more or less busy, if that was the case.

EXERCISE 3–1. *Continued*

	Daily Time Log	
Day of Week: M T W T F		Date:
Time	Activity	Comments
7:00		
7:30		
8:00		
8:30		
9:00		
9:30		
10:00		
10:30		
11:00		
11:30		
12:00		
12:30		
1:00		
1:30		
2:00		
2:30		
3:00		
3:30		
4:00		
4:30		
5:00		
5:30		

Was this day: _____ Typical?   Comments: _____
                          _____ More busy?   _____
                          _____ Less busy?   _____

EXERCISE 3–1. *Continued*

Daily Time Log		
Day of Week: M T W T F		Date:
Time	*Activity*	*Comments*
7:00		
7:30		
8:00		
8:30		
9:00		
9:30		
10:00		
10:30		
11:00		
11:30		
12:00		
12:30		
1:00		
1:30		
2:00		
2:30		
3:00		
3:30		
4:00		
4:30		
5:00		
5:30		

Was this day: _____ Typical?   Comments: _____
             _____ More busy?   _____
             _____ Less busy?   _____

EXERCISE 3–1. *Continued*

Daily Time Log		
Day of Week: M T W T F		Date:
Time	*Activity*	*Comments*
7:00		
7:30		
8:00		
8:30		
9:00		
9:30		
10:00		
10:30		
11:00		
11:30		
12:00		
12:30		
1:00		
1:30		
2:00		
2:30		
3:00		
3:30		
4:00		
4:30		
5:00		
5:30		

Was this day: _____ Typical?   Comments: _____
_____ More busy?   _____
_____ Less busy?   _____

EXERCISE 3–1. *Continued*

Daily Time Log		
Day of Week: M T W T F Date:		
Time	Activity	Comments
7:00		
7:30		
8:00		
8:30		
9:00		
9:30		
10:00		
10:30		
11:00		
11:30		
12:00		
12:30		
1:00		
1:30		
2:00		
2:30		
3:00		
3:30		
4:00		
4:30		
5:00		
5:30		

Was this day: _____ Typical?   Comments: _____
              _____ More busy?   _____
              _____ Less busy?   _____

EXERCISE 3–1. *Continued*

	Daily Time Log	
Day of Week: M T W T F		Date:
Time	*Activity*	*Comments*
7:00		
7:30		
8:00		
8:30		
9:00		
9:30		
10:00		
10:30		
11:00		
11:30		
12:00		
12:30		
1:00		
1:30		
2:00		
2:30		
3:00		
3:30		
4:00		
4:30		
5:00		
5:30		

Was this day: _____ Typical?   Comments: _____
                _____ More busy?   _____
                _____ Less busy?   _____

ANALYZING THE WAY YOU USE YOUR TIME

Using your Time Log as a basis, draw some conclusions and record them in response to the following questions.

1. Which part of your day seems to be most productive? Which part is least productive and why?

   _____

   _____

   _____

   _____

   _____

   _____

   _____

   _____

2. What recurring patterns of inefficiency—such as waiting for something, searching for something, or interruptions—do you observe?

   _____

   _____

   _____

   _____

   _____

   _____

   _____

3. What things are you doing that may be questionable in their necessity? These are only prospects for further scrutiny later.

   _____

   _____

   _____

   _____

   _____

4. What things are you doing that may be questionable in their appropriateness? Again, these are only prospects for further scrutiny.

_____

_____

_____

_____

_____

_____

5. Where do opportunities for increased efficiency exist?

_____

_____

_____

_____

_____

_____

6. What occasions do you find where you let enjoyment in doing a task override its priority?

_____

_____

_____

_____

_____

7. Did all of the activities you engaged in this week contribute to achieving an objective within an identified area of responsibility? If not, how do you justify spending time on the activity? Can this be changed in the future?

_____

_____

_____

_____

_____

8. On the average, what percentage of the time are you productive? What is your reaction to this figure?

_____

_____

_____

_____

_____

IN RETROSPECT

Reflect upon the ideas presented in this section and the results of your Time Log Analysis. Consider them within the context of your present job and work environment.

1. Does opportunity exist for you to make better use of your time? If so, where are the opportunities? If not, why not?

_____

_____

_____

_____

_____

_____

_____

2. What do you see as the major roadblocks to your using your time more effectively and efficiently?

_____

_____

_____

_____

_____

_____

_____

3. If you were successful in freeing up a few hours a week, how would you use that time and how would you avoid reverting to your present pattern of behavior?

_____

_____

_____

_____

_____

_____

_____

_____

4. Does your supervisor/manager support your objective to make better use of your time? What do you need to do to either gain or maintain appropriate support?

_____

_____

_____

_____

_____

_____

_____

_____

_____

_____

_____

5. Go back over your Time Log and fill in the actual percentage of time devoted to each area of responsibility on your Job Responsibility Analysis in Section 2. What is your reaction to the comparison between your estimated, ideal, and actual time distributions?

_____

_____

_____

_____

_____

_____

_____

_____

_____

_____

Delegation—Working Through Others

OBJECTIVES

- **Identify work you are presently doing that you should delegate.**
- **Determine to whom that work should be delegated.**
- **Understand the process of delegating and how to carry it out successfully.**
- **Recognize which members of your work group need more training to prepare them for further delegation.**
- **Understand the benefits of delegation.**

To delegate or not to delegate is never the question. To get everything done, you must make effective use of this tool. It is the only means available to broaden your span of influence beyond your own ability to personally do the work.

Why Some People Don't Delegate

Many reasons are offered to justify a lack of delegation. Some represent a valid concern such as a temporary staff shortage or lack of an adequately trained staff. Other reasons are of questionable validity. For example, some people may feel they are less capable than others and fear the consequences of being out performed. This insecurity leads them to carefully guard their jobs. Others may have the problem of perfectionism. These people feel the only way to get something done right is to do it themselves. Others simply enjoy doing the work to the extent that they are reluctant to fully let go. This is particularly true when people get promoted to supervise work they previously performed.

It's a bit unfair to assume that the nondelegating person is always the one at fault. You may have a manager who expects you to know every detail of what's going on in the section. When this happens, it is difficult, if not impossible, to delegate. Also, some staff members may resist accepting more responsibilities because of their own insecurities or lack of motivation. To check your views on delegation, complete Exercise 4–1.

EXERCISE 4–1. Self-Assessment in the Art of Delegation

Instructions: Read the following statements and circle the number to the right that reflects the degree to which each statement describes you.

	Strongly Agree				Strongly Disagree
1. The jobs I delegate never seem to get done the way I want them to be done.	5	4	3	2	1
2. I don't have the time to delegate properly.	5	4	3	2	1
3. I check on work without my staff knowing it so I can correct mistakes before they cause too many problems.	5	4	3	2	1
4. When I give clear instructions and work isn't done properly, I get upset.	5	4	3	2	1
5. My staff lack the commitment that I have, so work I delegate doesn't get done as well as I'd do it.	5	4	3	2	1
6. I can do the work of my section better than my staff can.	5	4	3	2	1
7. If the person I delegate work to doesn't do it well, I'll be severely criticized.	5	4	3	2	1
8. If I delegated everything I could, my job wouldn't be nearly as much fun.	5	4	3	2	1
9. When I delegate work, I often have to do it over.	5	4	3	2	1
10. I delegate clearly and concisely, explaining just how the job should be done.	5	4	3	2	1
11. When I delegate I lose control.	5	4	3	2	1
12. I could delegate more if my staff had more experience.	5	4	3	2	1

EXERCISE 4–1. *Continued*

	Strongly Agree				Strongly Disagree
13. I delegate routine tasks but keep the nonroutine work myself.	5	4	3	2	1
14. My manager expects me to be very close to all details of the work.	5	4	3	2	1
15. I have not found that delegation saves me time.	5	4	3	2	1
Column totals	——	——	——	——	——

Total score (all columns): ____

Scoring

Score can range from 15 to 75. Compare your score to the following:

75–60	You are failing to fully utilize your staff.
59–45	You can substantially improve your use of delegation.
44–30	You have some room for improvement as a delegator.
29–15	You are an excellent delegator or you fudged.

Adapted from "How to Improve Delegation Habits," by Theodore J. Krein, *Management Review,* May 1982, p. 59. ©1982 by AMACON, a division of American Management Associations, New York. Reprinted by permission of the publisher. All rights reserved.

Levels of Delegation

The goal in the delegation process is to have each staff member a self-sufficient person operating independent of you when carrying out day-to-day activities. Therefore, they should have the knowledge, skills, responsibilities, and authorities to handle a defined unit of work. The employee should be expected to make all relevant, routine decisions such as rate of work, quality of work, inventory levels of supplies or materials used, and when others need to be called in—such as maintenance personnel or extra help to meet deadlines.

Obviously, you can't bring someone into your section and immediately turn a part of your operation completely over to him or her. It takes time to get there. It takes time for the individual to acquire the knowledge and skills required to work at that level of delegation. It also takes time for you to develop confidence in his or her willingness and ability to take on the full range of duties and perform them according to appropriate standards. Therefore, full delegation becomes a target, or goal, to work toward.

Two concepts, used together, help lay out an approach to reach the goal of full delegation. The first one is identifying three distinct levels of delegation:

- Level 1—Delegate by what is to be done and how to do it but leave the employee some degree of freedom on rate of work and quality control.
- Level 2—Delegate by what is to be done but leave the employee free to decide how to do it, at what rate, and within what quality range.
- Level 3—Delegate by what is to be achieved but leave the employee free to decide what to do to get there, how to do it, at what rate, and within what quality range.

The second concept, which contributes, is noting a range of task involvement (see Figure 4–1).

When these two concepts are merged, it becomes clear that at each level of delegation there is opportunity for you to exercise from 100% to 0% of the control and influence on what is to be done and how it is to be done. In fact, preceding Level 1 delegation you have the opportunity to direct what, how, when, and at what rate and then inspect for quality each item of work completed.

Level 1 Delegation. This is the beginning point on the way to full delegation. This level is appropriate for employees who are unfamiliar with the full scope of job responsibilities. The actual delegation is limited to the rate, or pace, of work and decisions on acceptable levels of quality—that is, whether work measures up to a minimum quality level.

Within this level you may tell someone what is to be done and how to do it. For example, you might say: "John, I have been going over your shift reports, and I see that we are losing a lot of production time with machines being down for repairs. Now, I want you to catch as many of these problems as you can before they cause a machine to go down. To do that, I want you to review the maintenance log on each of your machines. Those that have gone 750 hours without maintenance are to be checked for proper lubrication and signs of vibration. Those that have gone

	Directive			Participative					Delegative		
Supervisor	100%	90	80	70	60	50	40	30	20	10	0%
Employee	0%	10	20	30	40	50	60	70	80	90	100%

FIGURE 4–1. Range of control and influence

1,200 hours or more are to be scheduled for shutdown during the next week for a maintenance check. Now to do that, call Betty in maintenance and set up a schedule. . . ."

Moving toward the other end of the control and influence range, you might tell a staff member what is to be done but allow him or her to offer suggestions on how to do it. As a result, your discussion culminates in an agreement between you and the individual on how the work will be done. The above situation might unfold as follows: "John, I have been going over your shift reports, and I see that we have been losing a lot of production time with machines being down for repairs. Now, I want us to catch as many of these problems as we can before they cause a machine to go down. What ideas do you have on how we can do that?"

After operating at this level for a while, the employee's capability should be clearly established. When the ability and willingness to take on more responsibility have been demonstrated, it is appropriate to move to the next level of delegation.

Level 2 Delegation. Moving to this level provides greater freedom and opportunity for work group members. This level of delegation is appropriate for those with demonstrated capability. Delegation at this level allows the employee to decide how things are to be done, at what pace in order to meet deadlines, and whether or not the work meets quality standards.

Within this level you again have a full range of control and influence available. But it is limited to decisions about what to do. Note: A supervisor may operate at different levels of delegation with the same employee on different portions of the employee's job. You may tell an employee what to do, you may discuss with an employee and decide between you what to do, or you may ask an employee what to do but reserve the right of approval or confirmation before it becomes an actual course of action.

An example of a discussion at this level of delegation where the supervisor exercises a high percentage of control and influence would be something like the following: "John, I have been going over your shift reports and see that we are losing a lot of production time with machines being down for repairs. Now, I want you to set up some kind of surveillance program on your machines to catch as many of these problems as you can before they actually cause a machine to go down. After you've given it some thought, let me know what you plan to do."

In this situation the supervisor exercises maximum control and influence within this level of delegation. The problem is pointed out, what to do about it is specified, and approval of the employee's plan is reserved. Yet, within this fairly restricted situation, the employee has the opportunity to study the situation, develop a plan to resolve the problem, and sell the supervisor on the merits of the plan.

The other extreme on the range of control and influence might be handled as follows: "John, I have been going over your shift reports and see that we are losing a lot of production time with machines being down for repairs. What can we do to cut down on this loss?"

Again, you would operate at this level long enough to establish your confidence in the employee's ability and willingness to perform at appropriate standards of performance. When this has been achieved, it's time to move to Level 3 delegation.

Level 3 Delegation.   This should be your goal—to get all of your staff to the point of handling their day-to-day responsibilities without your involvement. This level of delegation is appropriate when employees demonstrate a high level of ability and willingness to perform. Because of the level of ability and willingness required to perform successfully at this level of delegation, there are two reasons that may prevent your attaining this goal with all of your staff:

- Turnover within the group may keep you toward the low end of the job experience range.
- Some individuals will lack either the sense of responsibility or self-confidence required to achieve this level of delegation.

At Level 3 the staff member is given an area of responsibility and the freedom to make decisions within that area. There is still opportunity to discuss and direct or confirm the goals or objectives to be achieved. But beyond that, the employee decides what to do and how to do it. Furthermore, you must support those decisions after they have been made, whether you believe they are the best ones or not. Therefore, you must be willing to give up some of your authority and be willing to gamble that your staff can do a better job when left alone than when closely supervised.

As you progress through this level to the goal of full delegation, you can vary your degree of control and influence. However, characteristic of this level is the focus on what is to be achieved. This leaves the staff member free to determine what to do and how to do it in order to achieve the agreed-upon results.

How to Delegate

Delegation is both personal and individual. Doing it successfully depends to a large measure on the relationship between you and your staff as well as each staff member's abilities and interest. Still, some guidelines must be followed for delegation to be effective.

Communicate Fully.   When discussing work assignments, communicate fully the degrees of freedom and judgment you expect the other person to exercise. Also, you should share all the relevant information you have about the topic under discussion so your experience and knowledge can be utilized. Finally, engage the other person in the conversation in order to confirm his or her understanding of your point of view.

Delegate Authority as Well as Responsibility.   Your staff must have the authority to carry out the responsibilities they have been delegated. Within most organizations this means authority to spend money and take necessary personnel actions in pursuit of objectives. This authority may appropriately be specified within certain limits. For example, you may grant authority to purchase outside goods and services within approved budget. You may grant authority to authorize overtime to meet production deadlines within some specified limit, such as not to exceed 10% of scheduled hours. When you delegate responsibilities without authority, you are maintaining control too tightly and, in the process, demonstrating a lack of trust in staff members.

Set Performance Standards.   Performance standards are a significant part of effective delegation. Your staff must know the outcomes you expect. They can appropriately have a hand in developing the standards but should not be given an assignment without agreement from you on relevant standards of performance. Standards typically cover such areas as quality, quantity, timeliness, and costs.

Establish Controls.   You don't cut your staff loose and say, "Okay, you're on your own. Go to it." You must establish controls that let you know progress is being made toward the agreed-upon outcome and alert you to problems that may crop up to impede progress. The following techniques are available to you:

- *Personal Inspection.*   When a tangible product is the output of your group, conduct periodic inspections of product quality and operating procedures.
- *Client Feedback.*   Occasionally, ask your clients or customers about the performance of your group.
- *Visual Displays.*   Keep charts and graphs of actual results against planned results to monitor deviation from plan.
- *Computer Printouts.*   Tie into computer-based financial systems, personnel systems, production systems, etc., to generate reports of actual vs planned results.
- *Status Reports.*   Ask staff members to provide periodic reports on progress and problems anticipated. These reports can be oral or written. Oral reports can be handled privately or in a group setting.

Challenge Your Staff.   Some supervisors tend to play it safe and not allow their staff too much responsibility or latitude in decision making. Under these conditions people do not develop to their full potential. They need challenge, not restriction.

To fully develop your staff, you should tend toward overdelegation rather than underdelegation. This will create some anxiety because some members will be unsure of their ability to handle the responsibility they've been given. However, most will be able to accept the challenge and will grow in the process.

Provide Appropriate Training.   Training and coaching are the means available to you for developing your staff to their full capabilities. You cannot expect employees to join your group fully trained and ready to assume full responsibility.

Training may come from you, experienced members of your staff, professional instructors, and individual study. It provides the basic knowledge and skills required to get the job done. When handled well, it also bolsters self-confidence and creates an interest in doing the work. Training is an essential part of the developmental process.

Coaching comes only from you, the supervisor. It is the appropriate next step following training. It involves observing the work of the employee, answering questions, correcting errors in work performance, and reinforcing correct performance. It is most effective when handled in a supportive, encouraging way.

Support Your Staff. An essential ingredient of effective delegation is to support, or back, your staff in the decisions they make when the decision responsibility has been appropriately delegated. This won't always be easy. At times you will honestly believe you could do it better than your staff. But to be an effective delegator, you must be willing to accept the risk.

For most supervisors to accept this restriction, some realistic limitations must be acknowledged. When the decision represents greater risk than you are willing to accept, you obviously can intervene. But be careful. Don't do this very often; when you do, explain the dangers you foresee and involve the staff member in developing an alternative course of action.

When the risk is within an acceptable tolerance, let the decision run its course and then engage in an analysis of the situation. This allows your staff to learn by doing, which is certainly the most effective means available. During this analysis, involve the individual in generating other possible courses of action and evaluating them so that in the future the number of possible response options to choose from will be greater. Then give the staff member another chance.

Delegate; Don't Dump. As you consider the work you are presently doing, delegate those things that will result in a more complete job assignment for staff members. The job should provide meaningful and challenging duties that logically fit together. Avoid the tendency to dump all of the unpleasant duties associated with your job while retaining all of the interesting ones. The following items become prospects for delegation:

- Work that is reoccurring—save your time for the unique events.
- Work that you are least qualified to handle—use the talent available to you.
- Work that demands the greatest portion of your time—free up your schedule to be more readily available.
- Work that narrows your area of specialization—good managers and supervisors do not need to be super technicians.

Don't Abdicate Responsibility. You must not abdicate your responsibility as supervisor. You are accountable to your manager for the results of your unit and must exercise prudent judgment in achieving those results. Delegation does not mean letting an aggressive staff member, regardless of how capable he or she may be, take over the operation. You can delegate without fear as long as you stay in charge. Staff members must understand that their authority derives from you and it can be recalled as quickly as it was delegated, if they begin to overreach the agreed upon limits of their authority.

To be able to exercise full responsibility, you must be aware of all that gets done within your unit and be interested in it being done well. Don't ignore certain areas because you lack interest in them.

Benefits of Delegation

The most obvious benefit of delegation is the time that is freed up for you to do the things only you can do. When each member of your staff is assigned a significant part of your unit's work and is carrying it out successfully, you should be able to get most of your work done during regular hours rather than taking it home with you. The activities you can spend time on include:

- Planning the future of your unit. Rather than operating from crisis to crisis, you look further ahead and determine both where you want to be and how to get there.
- Developing new and better techniques for doing the work of your unit as well as developing new areas of involvement.
- Representing your group, and its individual members, to higher management. For example, do other appropriate managers know the qualifications and capabilities of your staff?
- Establishing better relationships with other groups with whom you deal on a regular basis. Effort in this area is frequently required in order to ensure cooperation and support from others.
- Building and maintaining relationships with your staff. It takes time to talk to people and develop the depth of relationships that ensure cohesiveness in a group. This time is frequently lost when a supervisor is "too" busy.
- Coordinating the work of your unit for optimum productivity. You need to avoid duplication of effort as well as make sure certain things are not neglected. You need to see that those who can contribute to a common task are aware of the opportunity to contribute.

Getting Started

To get started on the path to increased delegation, analyze your personal involvement in the work of your unit (Exercise 4–2). In this analysis, sort all the work you do into three categories:

1. Work that can be delegated immediately.
2. Work that can be delegated as soon as someone is trained to take it over.
3. Work that can only be done by you either because of company policy or directive from management.

Now consider the members of your staff. How ready are they for delegation? Consider two things—their ability to do the work and their interest in doing it well. Have they ever had the opportunity to do these things before? If so, what was the outcome?

Work you are now doing that can be delegated immediately should be assigned to staff members in accordance with the currently appropriate level of delegation. Then, as you acquire confidence in the individual's ability, you should increase the delegation until you have accomplished as near complete delegation as possible.

You already have freed up some of your time. This provides you the opportunity to address Category 2. Select the staff members who are to be trained to take on additional responsibilities. These are the ones to be trained either by you, someone else on your staff, or someone from the training department. As soon as they are properly prepared, proceed to delegate by degree until you have achieved full delegation.

If anyone demonstrates a lack of interest in an increased level of delegation, provide work assignments with clear performance expectations, then follow up with feedback on performance. Through this process establish a success cycle. Nothing creates interest faster than success—achievement, recognition, reinforcement.

Finally, when increasing the level of delegation to your staff, consider their present workload and level of responsibility. It may be necessary to reassign work within the unit, assign work to staff support groups, or discontinue certain work. Also, the benefits of adding an additional staff member to enhance the overall contribution of the group shouldn't be overlooked.

Don't overlook your secretary. In many cases secretaries are restricted to typing, filing, and running errands. When this is the case, a great deal of potential is wasted. The best approach is to view your secretary as a partner in getting your job accomplished. Whether you have a private secretary or share one with other members of your work group, the two of you can work effectively together.

Delegate to your secretary the same way you do to other members of your staff. Look especially for opportunities where she or he can make decisions for you and carry out completed tasks without your involvement. One example might be scheduling your appointments. Here your secretary would determine the appropriateness of a requested appointment and when it could be scheduled, and then simply advise you of it. Another example might be handling your mail. Routine requests for information would be handled without your involvement. Your secretary could even sign the letter. Other replies to correspondence could be written, ready for your signature. Beyond scheduling and correspondence, look for opportunities in data gathering, data analysis, and records keeping.

To assess the opportunities to better utilize your secretary, complete Exercise 4–3.

EXERCISE 4–2. Planning for Improved Delegation

Category 1—Work That Can Be Delegated Immediately

Task or Activity   *Delegate To:*   *Level*

1. _____
2. _____
3. _____
4. _____
5. _____
6. _____

Category 2—Work to Delegate after Training

Task or Activity   *Delegate To:*

1. _____
2. _____
3. _____
4. _____
5. _____
6. _____

What steps are necessary to accomplish the delegations listed above?

Step 1. _____

_____

_____   Target date:_____

Step 2. _____

_____

_____   Target date:_____

Step 3. _____

_____

_____   Target date:_____

Step 4. _____

_____

_____   Target date:_____

EXERCISE 4–2. *Continued*

Category 3—Work That Can Only Be Done by You

1. _____
2. _____
3. _____
4. _____
5. _____
6. _____

From the above list, identify any items you would like to delegate but will have to change either policy or your manager's directive before delegation can be accomplished.

1. _____
2. _____
3. _____

What steps are necessary to accomplish the delegations listed above?

Step 1. _____

_____

_____ Target date:_____

Step 2. _____

_____

_____ Target date:_____

Step 3. _____

_____

_____ Target date:_____

Step 4. _____

_____

_____ Target date:_____

EXERCISE 4–3. How Well Do I Utilize My Secretary?

Your response to the following 15 questions will help you evaluate your effectiveness. For each question circle the score that applies to you. Then total your score and rate yourself at the end of the exercise.

	Often	Sometimes	Rarely
1. Do you delegate as much as you can to your secretary?	2	0	−1
2. Do you do things on the basis of their priority?	2	1	−1
3. Do you discuss your secretary's career goals with her (him) on a periodic basis?	2	0	−1
4. Do you open your own mail?	−1	0	2
5. Do you demand perfection in the work efforts of your secretary?	−1	0	2
6. Do you switch work priorities on your secretary?	−1	1	2
7. Do you interrupt your secretary while she (he) is working?	−1	1	2
8. Do you utilize your secretary as effectively as you can to help solve your time problems?	2	0	−1
9. Do you use your secretary as a sounding board for ideas and problem solving?	2	0	−1
10. Do you have confidence in your secretary to handle routine activities?	2	0	−1
11. Do you surprise your secretary with rush jobs late in the day?	−1	1	2
12. When out of the office, do you keep your secretary informed as to where you can be reached?	2	1	−1

EXERCISE 4–3. *Continued*

	Often	Sometimes	Rarely
13. Do you compliment your secretary on work well done?	2	0	−1
14. Do you allow your secretary to suggest new ideas for doing things?	2	0	−1
15. Do you and your secretary review daily objectives each morning?	2	0	−1
Column totals	____	____	____

Total score (all three columns): ____

Scores can range between 30 and −15. A score below 15 suggests that you are not utilizing your secretary effectively.

From *Effective Time Management for Managers,* Charles L. Scott, p. 17, © 1978. Used by permission of the author. All rights reserved.

Summary and Conclusions

In the eyes of some critics of modern business practices, much of the meaning has been taken out of jobs. Employee talents, skills, and abilities lie fallow because of bureaucratic constraints. What can be done to remedy this situation? Delegate! Delegate responsibility, authority, and accountability for a meaningful segment of your unit's work to each member of your staff.

You benefit from delegation by having time to address the higher-order management duties, which often get neglected. These include long-range planning, innovation, coordination both within your group and with other units of your organization, and representing your work group and its members to higher management. These things just don't get done well when you are heavily involved in the day-to-day work of your group.

Your goal, in delegating, is to have each member of your staff operating independent of you in routine matters. To attain this goal, you need to delegate by degrees, or levels. This allows for the development of both your and your staff members' confidence in getting the job done according to your expectations. There are risks involved in delegating; they are a necessary part of the process. But they can be kept in bounds by moving slowly toward your goal.

Delegation has been characterized as giving staff members plenty of rope but making sure they do not hang themselves. This means you need to provide the necessary training for them to be able to do the delegated work. It also means that you must provide an environment where they feel at ease coming to you when the going gets tough or a decision has failed. They also need to know that they must keep you informed—because of your mutual interest in what's going on, not because you are the boss peering over their shoulders.

IN RETROSPECT

1. Describe the extent of delegation in your work group. Consider both delegation from your manager to you and from you to members of your staff.

   _____

   _____

   _____

   _____

   _____

   _____

   _____

   _____

   _____

   _____

2. What, in your opinion, is preventing the attainment of full delegation in your work group, if it has not yet been achieved?

   _____

   _____

   _____

   _____

   _____

   _____

   _____

   _____

   _____

   _____

3. Reflect on the discussion of delegation presented in the text. What new ideas did you receive? How can the concepts presented be used to improve performance in your work group?

_____

_____

_____

_____

_____

_____

_____

_____

_____

Section 5.

Planning—Key to Achievement

OBJECTIVES

- **Emphasize the importance of taking time to plan.**
- **Present several techniques, or planning aids, to help you in the planning process.**
- **Examine the potential application of improved planning to your area of responsibility.**

Planning is an interesting process. Some people are good at it while others aren't. Some are so caught up in activities and deadlines that they believe they do not have time to plan. Yet, planning holds the key for relieving the stress of too little time. It is the way to structure your own future and, as such, becomes the key to achievement.

Planning makes two basic contributions that help bring order to your life. First, it lets you know the steps to take to get from where you are to where you want to be. Second, it tells you what resources will be required to get there. Thus, the two typically limiting resources of time and money must be reckoned with. As a result, you know when to begin something in order to be able to complete it on schedule, and you know what it is going to cost.

Planning typically takes place within two time horizons—long-term and short-term. Long-term plans look at what you expect to accomplish during the next year as well as what is required to complete a particular project. A project's duration may be more or less than a year. When it exceeds a week, it falls on the long-term horizon. Short-term plans look at what you expect to accomplish this week and today. These may be either steps toward longer-term objectives or tasks that are complete in and of themselves.

Long-Term Planning

Long-term planning begins with a clear statement of objective. Next is a determination of the means by which you will attain the objective. This may be a very demanding part of the process as you search out a way to achieve a particular objective within the constraints that exist. At this step in the process the original optimistic objective may have to be modified somewhat in order to move into the realm of realism.

Programming.   With an objective and a means to attain it determined, the next step is to program the action steps required to make it happen. Programming involves a detailing of the tasks and activities required to move the project forward. A certain amount of discretion and judgment is called for in determining how minute to break down the various tasks. The important guidelines are meaningful steps, to be taken by one person, that are critical to moving ahead on the project.

Scheduling.   From programming you move to scheduling. This activity involves two issues: First, estimating the time required to carry out each task and activity and, second, determining the appropriate sequence of events. Typically, from this activity also comes a decision on what steps, if any, can be underway at the same time.

Scheduling must focus on calendar time involved. It records the number of days required to complete an action step or the target date by which a step will be completed. It is not reported out in terms of actual hours or days of effort required. An estimate of actual time is a logical starting point in determining your schedule. But this estimate is then considered along with all of the other demands placed upon the person responsible for completing the action step. Considering the priority of this task along with others leads to a schedule for completing the activity.

From scheduling comes the beginning date of a project in order to be able to complete it by the target date stated in the original objective. This becomes one of the major contributions of planning—to let you know when something must be started in order to complete it by the due date. How often have you casually estimated the amount of time required on a project only to find when you got into it more time was required than was available? At that point the only alternative was to be late. Careful planning will help you reduce the number of times you are caught short in this manner.

Planning Aids.   Three common methods for working up and presenting plans are the worksheet format, Gantt chart, and PERT diagram (Exhibits 5–1, 5–2, and 5–3, respectively). The worksheet is preferred when there are no concurrent steps involved. It has the added advantage of showing cost estimates and assigned responsibility for the various steps. Gantt charts and PERT diagrams clearly show what can be underway at the same time. PERT diagrams have the added advantage of demonstrating the time-critical activities in order to complete the project on schedule.

Regardless of which charting method you choose, the due date of each action step should be entered on your master calendar. When others are responsible for a critical step in your plan, you should enter a follow-up date on your calendar a few days before the due date.

Planning aids are a critical part of effective time management. One simply cannot remember everything that must be done by when. Select from the alternatives available the planning aids that fit the type of work you do and appeal to you. Then use them to bring order to your life. One word of caution: Don't get caught up in too elaborate charting techniques. You may find you spend more time filling in planning aids than appropriate.

EXHIBIT 5–1. Action Planning Worksheet

Objective:

Action Step	Target Date	Cost		Assigned Responsibility
		Dollars	Time	

EXHIBIT 5–2. Example of Gantt Chart

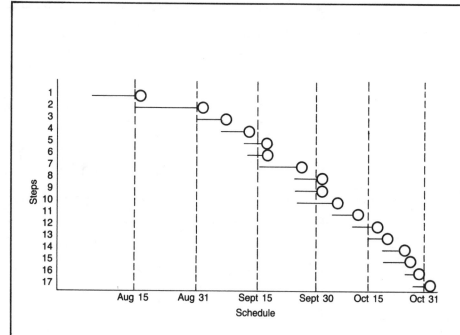

Note: When a step is completed, color in the circle at the end of the line representing that step on the chart.

Steps in Project

1. Draw working plans
2. Obtain building permit
3. Form and pour foundation
4. Frame walls and roof
5. Install roofing
6. Install windows
7. Install exterior siding
8. Paint exterior
9. Install electrical wiring
10. Install heating/air conditioning
11. Insulate
12. Install sheetwork
13. Paint interior
14. Install interior doors and trim
15. Install electrical fixtures
16. Clean up
17. Install floor covering

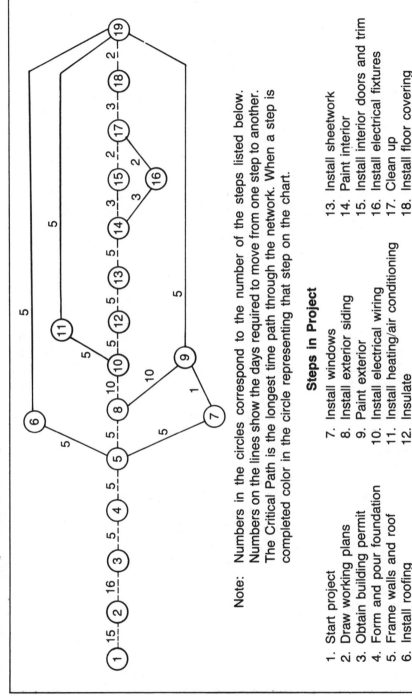

EXHIBIT 5–3. Example of PERT Diagram

Note: Numbers in the circles correspond to the number of the steps listed below. Numbers on the lines show the days required to move from one step to another. The Critical Path is the longest time path through the network. When a step is completed color in the circle representing that step on the chart.

Steps in Project

1. Start project
2. Draw working plans
3. Obtain building permit
4. Form and pour foundation
5. Frame walls and roof
6. Install roofing
7. Install windows
8. Install exterior siding
9. Paint exterior
10. Install electrical wiring
11. Install heating/air conditioning
12. Insulate
13. Install sheetwork
14. Paint interior
15. Install interior doors and trim
16. Install electrical fixtures
17. Clean up
18. Install floor covering
19. Project completion

Short-Term Planning

Action steps in your long-term plans get integrated and prioritized with other demands as you develop your short-term plans. Short-term plans are best developed and scheduled on a weekly and daily basis.

Weekly Plans. A weekly plan looks at what you want to have accomplished by the end of the week and the activities necessary to do that. Weekly plans can be developed late on Friday for the following week, over the weekend, or early Monday morning. Many people use commuting time to plan their week and day.

Worksheets for weekly plans can take a variety of forms. Exhibit 5–4 can serve as a starting place to develop your own or can be copied and used. When filled in, the worksheet should be kept handy for frequent reference, and the daily activities should be transferred to your calendar. These activities then flow naturally into your daily plans and take their place according to assigned priorities.

Daily Plans. The culmination of the planning process is to let you know what has to be done today. If you have kept your calendar up to date, the majority of your daily activities will already be recorded. This is the obvious starting place to develop your list of things to do today.

A list of things to do today, in priority order, can be a valuable aid in focusing your energy on the most important demands facing you each morning. Start at the top of your list. Recognize that unexpected demands will come up. Caution: Assess their priority and handle them accordingly. Don't use an unexpected demand as an excuse to take you away from your list! When the unexpected has been dealt with— either by completing it, adding it to your list, or giving it to someone—return to your list. At the end of the day carry forward any items remaining on your list and reprioritize them along with new items for tomorrow.

The value of a "To Do" list is illustrated in a story. The president of a large steel company hired a management consultant to work with the top executives of the firm in an effort to improve their effectiveness. After meeting with each executive, the consultant reported back to the president. His recommendation was that each executive keep a daily list of things to do in priority order and devote as much time as possible to completing the list each day. Any items remaining at the end of the day were to be carried forward and reprioritized along with tomorrow's activities. The consultant did not bill the firm for his services. Rather, he told the president to try the recommendation for a few weeks and then send a check for whatever he considered the recommendation to be worth. About a month later the consultant received a check from the firm for $25,000.

The format for your list is not important. It can be written on your calendar, on a plain sheet of paper, or on a special form. (Many business stationery stores have a variety of stock planning forms to choose from.) Exhibit 5–5 illustrates the simplicity recommended. A more detailed example is shown as Exhibit 5–6.

EXHIBIT 5–4.   Weekly Planning Worksheet

Objectives:

1. _____

2. _____

3. _____

Activities	Priority	Estimated Time	Day

EXHIBIT 5–5. Things to Do Today

(Number in Priority Order)

From your To Do list you can lay out a daily schedule. This should reflect meetings, appointments, and appropriate blocks of private time to accomplish the high-priority items on your list.

When considering your daily schedule, keep your personal energy cycle in mind (Figure 5–1). Some people are at their best early in the morning. Others peak in the mid or late morning. Plan your daily schedule to match your prime time as much as possible. You will not always have complete control but consider such simple ideas as reading and responding to your mail or returning phone calls after lunch rather than early in the morning when such activity would impinge on your prime time. Chart your typical energy cycle in Exercise 5–1.

What to Do When Things Don't Go as Planned

At times even the best-developed plans will not work out. When these occasions arise, it is helpful to have contingency plans available. Contingency plans can be developed by addressing three questions:

- What is likely to go wrong?
- When will I know about it?
- What can I do about it?

EXHIBIT 5–6.   Things to Do Today

		Date:
Tasks to Complete	Done	Appointments to Keep
		7:00
		8:00
		9:00
		10:00
		11:00
		12:00
Phone Calls to Make	Done	
		1:00
		2:00
		3:00
People to See	Done	4:00
		5:00
		6:00
		7:00

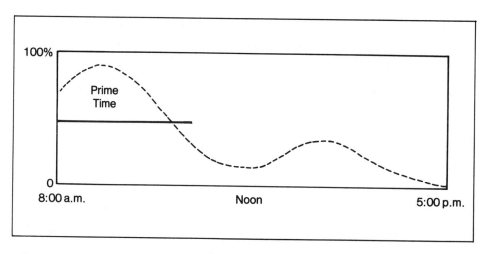

FIGURE 5–1. Typical energy cycle

EXERCISE 5–1. Your Energy Cycle

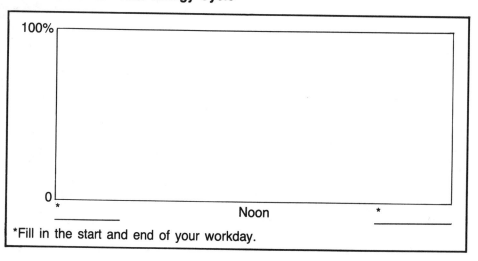

Each of these questions can be addressed in terms of the four classic control elements—quality, quantity, cost, and timeliness. All situations have at least a timeliness dimension for contingency planning. Other situations may include one, two, or all three of the remaining ones. Figure 5–2 summarizes the rather limited range of response to failure to meet deadlines and budgets.

Response Options	Control Element	
	Timeliness	Cost
1. Renegotiate	X	X
2. Recover from subsequent steps	X	X
3. Narrow scope of project	X	X
4. Deploy more resources (manpower/ machinery)	X	
5. Accept substitution for unavailable parts	X	X
6. Seek alternative sources of parts or supplies	X	X
7. Accept partial delivery	X	
8. Offer incentives	X	
9. Demand compliance with agreements	X	X

FIGURE 5–2. Response options

Summary and Conclusions

Planning is the way of moving from a reactive mode to a proactive one. It is the key to structuring your own future and thereby becomes the key to achievement.

The extent and nature of planning needs to be adapted to individual circumstances. The three-part process laid out in this section may be too elaborate for your particular situation. For example, your list of things to do today may have only one item on it. If that's the case, you probably can remember one item without writing it down. However, if you have many things to do, a list will be very helpful.

Your approach to planning should recognize two time horizons—long-term and short-term. The division between these two horizons used in this section was simply more than a week and a week or less. You should look at the particular nature of your job and define these two terms more precisely for your situation. A month might be a better breakpoint. The outer limit of the long-term horizon is defined by the lead time required to get to an objective within your assigned area of responsibility.

All planning should be done with acknowledging the conditions of uncertainty that apply. Recognize that the farther into the future plans are developed, the greater the degree of uncertainty. With this principle in mind, maintain as much flexibility as possible to take full advantage of new information and opportunities that develop as you pursue your plans.

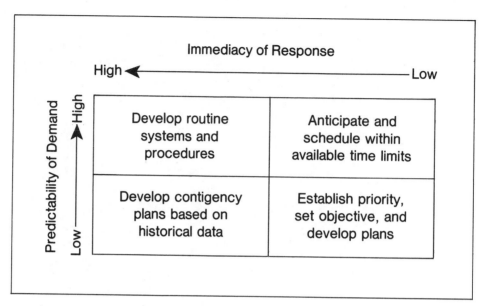

FIGURE 5–3. How to cope with job demands

IN RETROSPECT

Reflect upon the ideas presented in this section and consider them in the context of your present job and work environment.

1. To what extent do you plan your present activities? Where do opportunities exist for you to utilize better planning techniques?

_____

_____

_____

_____

2. Which of the planning aids do you currently use? Which ones could you take advantage of to bring more order to your area of responsibility? (Project planning worksheets, Gantt charts, PERT diagrams, weekly planning worksheets, daily lists of things to do)

_____

_____

_____

_____

_____

3. Within what time frames do you consider your long-term and short-term horizons to fall?

_____

_____

_____

_____

_____

_____

4. What types of events typically interfere with your carrying out your plans? How can contingency plans help you deal with some of these interferences?

_____

_____

_____

_____

_____

_____

5. How well does your work schedule conform to your energy cycle? How can you rearrange your schedule to make better use of your prime time?

_____

_____

_____

_____

_____

_____

Section 6.

Coping with Common Time Wasters

OBJECTIVES

- **Define what constitutes a time waster.**
- **Identify time wasters that impact you.**
- **Help you reduce or eliminate the interference in your day caused by time wasters.**

Everyone wastes time occasionally. This is especially true when you consider that you are wasting time whenever you spend time doing something less important than what you could otherwise be doing. The key questions, then, are: What else might you be doing? and, Is it of a higher priority? You are not necessarily wasting time when you take a break, converse with associates, talk on the telephone, or read a magazine. You are wasting time when you allow these activities to keep you away from higher priority ones.

Time wasters come from two general sources. One source is the environment in which you work. This is basically all of the things people do, or don't do, that end up wasting your time. The other source is yourself. This, of course, is all of the things you bring on yourself that end up wasting your time. In Exercise 6–1 list all the things you can think of from these two sources that impact your use of time.

Coping with Self-Generated Time Wasters

The most common self-generated time wasters fall into three categories—lack of organization, procrastination, and inability to say no. You may have others on your list. If so, perhaps discussing these three will give you some ideas on how to address the problems you personally face.

Disorganization. Disorganization leads to wasted time. It crops up in three situations: wasted effort due to a poor layout of the work area, wasted time spent searching for things, and wasted time due to starting and stopping a task perhaps two or three times before it is completed.

Look around your work area. How do you handle the normal tasks involved in carrying out your job? Your area should be laid out to minimize effort. There should be a free and normal flow of materials and movement. Consider the placement of equipment such as telephone and calculator, proximity of supplies that are frequently used, and accessibility of files.

The next focus of your attention should be on your desk or work table. Is your work area cluttered? How much time do you waste looking for things that you know

EXERCISE 6–1.   List of Time Wasters

Self	Environment

are there but just can't put your finger on them? When was the last time you used the various items in and on your desk? Perhaps a weekend of house-cleaning is in order.

The old axiom, "A place for everything and everything in its place," is the best advice for organizing your information. Set up files for work in progress and keep them in your desk. Keep everything relating to a particular project in its file folder. Set up files for your information and index the articles and reports contained therein for quick referral. Establish call-up files for items that need future action. Keep a file folder for current requests received either by mail, telephone, or personal visit. Make a note of all such requests and file them in this folder. Then, check it daily to see what needs to be done. Consider setting up a Master Control Book (See Exhibit 6–1).

Finally, organize, to the extent possible, your approach to your work. Practice task completion. If you are interrupted, do not immediately jump to a new task. First, assess the priority of the request. If at all possible, defer getting involved in the new activity until you've completed your current one. If the interruption comes by phone or personal visit, make a note to yourself to handle it later. Pay particular attention to a general tendency to respond to the rank of the one making the request rather than the importance of the request. Most people are willing to be reasonable about their demands on your time. Also, organize the contact you initiate with others (See Exhibit 6–2).

EXHIBIT 6–1. Master Control Book

Set up a master control book. This is any three-ring, loose-leaf binder to hold the plans, notes, checklists, and other information you need to get your job done. No longer do you have to rely on your memory—just flip to the appropriate section when you need to check some detail.

In time, you can develop your own layout to fit your individual needs. However, to get started, consider the following five sections.

- *Section 1: Things to do.* In this section keep a copy of your weekly plans and daily things-to-do lists. Additional pages can be added for any supplementary notes you may need to make.

- *Section 2: Follow up.* Keep copies of your Project Record and/or Assignment Log in this section. Go over them daily or weekly to determine appropriate follow-up on projects in progress.

- *Section 3: Plans.* In this section keep copies of action planning worksheets, PERT diagrams, or Gantt charts, as appropriate, for all of your projects. This section can be supplemented with blank sheets of paper for appropriate notes on projects pending or underway.

- *Section 4: Checklists.* File in this section checklists on the various routine tasks you must do from time to time. This may include budget preparation procedures, equipment maintenance checklists, or account reconciliation procedures—just whatever your job demands. If you do not have these checklists available, consider developing them. They save time in the long run.

- *Section 5: Sample letters.* Why spend hours laboring over letters that you must write to make them clear, direct, and readable? Simply collect copies of correspondence that you receive, which you feel communicates effectively, and file it in this section. Then, the next time you are faced with writing a letter, flip through this section to get some good ideas.

From "Getting Organized," Rosalind Gold, *Supervisory Management*, p. 24, © 1983. Used by permission of author. All rights reserved.

EXHIBIT 6–1. *Continued*

	Project Record				
Priority	*Project*	*Date Assigned*	*Due Date*	*Done*

EXHIBIT 6–1. *Continued*

Assignment Log						
Project or Task	Date Assigned	Time Estimate	Due Date	Extended To	Date Completed	Remarks

EXHIBIT 6–2. Conference Planner

Instructions: Enter the names of those with whom you have frequent conferences. As you think of items you need to discuss with each, jot them down. When it is time for a conference, prioritize the list. Mark out relatively unimportant items or those that can be handled in some other way.

Name:	Name:	Name:

Name:	Name:	Name:

Name:	Name:	Name:

Procrastination. Sometimes you may put things off that you know should be done but for whatever reason you can't get interested in starting. Typically, this includes the boring, difficult, unpleasant, or onerous work to be done. (See Exercise 6–2 at the end of this section.) When this happens, consider the following ideas:

- Set a deadline for yourself to complete the task and stick with it.
- Set up a reward system. For example, "When I finish that task I'm going to buy myself a new _____." Or, "I'm not going to lunch until I finish this task."
- Arrange with someone—an associate or secretary—to follow up with you on your progress.
- Do the undesirable task first in the morning and be done with it.

Inability to Say No. In some cases the demands on your time exceed your ability to accommodate all of them. Here is where priorities and the ability to say no can come to your rescue. When you take on more than you can handle, quality usually begins to suffer. In the long term, you will be better off to take on only what you can handle well.

Saying no doesn't have to offend. When you can offer an alternative, things can usually be worked out to everyone's satisfaction. On the other hand, when a new demand comes in that is higher in priority to some of your current commitments, renegotiate the due dates on your current projects or have them reassigned to someone else.

Rather than saying yes too often, try some of these responses instead:

- I can take care of that, but in order to do so what I'm now doing will be delayed. Is what you're requesting more important?
- I'll be glad to take care of that for you. However, I can't get to it until I finish what I'm now doing. That will be . . .
- I'm sorry, I just don't have the time to take on any new work. I'll be glad to call you when my schedule frees up.
- I appreciate the compliment, but I just can't work it into my schedule at this time.
- I'm sorry, I can't, but you might consider . . .

Coping with Environmental Time Wasters

Even when you are well organized and trying to effectively use your time, you must contend with interruptions and distractions from others. (See Exercise 6–3 at the end of this section.) Here are some ideas for handling the most common ones.

Visitors. Controlling the time taken up by visitors requires both courtesy and good judgment. As a starting point, limit the number of people you invite to your work area. If you need to be with someone, go to his or her work place. This way you can control your time commitment by simply excusing yourself and leaving when you have accomplished your purpose. It is much more difficult to get people to leave your work area than it is for you to leave theirs.

You can head off a lot of drop-in visitors by turning your desk so your back is to the door. When people walk by and see that you are busy, they tend to not interrupt you unless it is important to do so. Next, consider closing your door, if you have a private office, when you need to concentrate on some task. Again, the casual drop-in will think twice before interrupting.

Finally, when someone drops in, stand up to talk. Don't invite your visitor to be seated unless you have time to spend in conversation. Usually, when you stand, your visitor will also remain standing. This will significantly limit the length of the conversation. If this does not work, just be tactful and honest with your visitor. Consider something like, "Thanks for dropping in. However, I really need to get this project finished."

Telephone Calls. For many, telephones are a constant interruption. You probably can't eliminate these interruptions. The best you can hope for is to limit the amount of time they use. If you have someone to answer your phone, you can screen out a few calls that should be handled by someone else and have calls taken during periods when you should not be interrupted.

When talking on the phone, do not initiate social conversation, unless both you and the other person have time for it. Do not go into unnecessary elaboration in response to questions. End the conversation when it has achieved its business purpose. Do this in a polite but firm way by saying, "Thanks for calling. I'm glad I could be of help" or, "Thanks for calling. I have something I must get back to."

Incoming Mail. A third way others enter your life making demands on your time is through the mail. Unsolicited mail arrives daily in an unending flood. If you have someone to sort your mail, give that person guidelines on what you want to see, what should be routed to others, and what should be immediately thrown out. Further sorting your mail into two categories, "information only" and "action required," would be helpful.

Establish a practice of handling each piece of mail only once. As you read it decide what action is required and then take that action. Information-only mail can be accumulated and read at times convenient to you. These times might include commuting, while waiting for appointments, while waiting for meetings to begin, over lunch, or in the evening.

You can save a lot of time responding to mail by telephoning with requested information, having someone else telephone and pass on the information, or writing a brief response in longhand on the original letter and mailing it back. If a record copy is needed, have the letter with your reply on it photocopied before it is mailed.

Waiting. How much time do you spend waiting each week—waiting for appointments, waiting for meetings to begin, waiting for others to complete something, waiting on airplanes, and waiting to get somewhere while traveling and commuting? A lot of opportunity exists to make better use of waiting time.

Waiting time need not be wasted time. Two approaches help convert it to productive time. First, don't spend an unreasonable amount of time waiting for others with whom you have appointments. If you go to someone's office but are not received promptly, leave word with a secretary to call you when you can be received and return to your office.

The other way to make productive use of waiting time is to use it to take care of other tasks. For example, return telephone calls and read your mail, including trade and professional journals. Also, you should always carry a tablet and pencil. Then you can use waiting time to develop plans or write letters. Finally, you can carry a file folder of small, low-priority things to do and use this time to do them. The availability of compact battery-operated cassette recorders can help improve your productivity during travel and commuting. Either listen to tapes of information to aid in your own development or use the machine to record ideas and instructions for use when you return to your office.

Meetings.   Time wasted in meetings needs to be examined from two points of view—the meetings you call and the meetings you attend.

When you call a meeting, know what you want to accomplish as a result of the meeting, get the minimum number of appropriate people together, lay out your agenda, and move into the purpose of the meeting. Have a time limit set for the meeting; otherwise, you have no base line for managing your time. Keep the discussion on topic, periodically summarize where you are, and test for decision from time to time. When a decision has been reached, assign responsibility and follow-up dates to convert the decision to action. Adjourn the meeting and release participants so they can move onto other responsibilities. Use Exhibit 6–3 to help you plan your meetings.

The most common violators of good meeting practices are the periodic staff meetings. In a vast number of cases they are a waste of time for many in attendance. Two suggestions will make significant improvements in these meetings. First, start off by setting an agenda. Simply ask, "What do we have to talk about today." If more material is generated than can be handled in the available time, prioritize your list. If nothing significant is offered, immediately adjourn the meeting. The second suggestion is to eliminate all discussion that involves only two participants. These should be handled as one-to-one sessions, not group sessions.

When you attend someone else's meeting, be sure it is necessary for you to be present. Then arrive on time, prepared to participate in the discussion; avoid taking the discussion off track or prolonging it. Cooperate with and support the one chairing the meeting to make it a productive experience. If you end up with a follow-up item from the meeting, add it to your list of things to do with its appropriate priority designation.

Crises.   Many people believe that crises are an unavoidable part of their jobs. That's only partly the case. The unique, unexpected event will occur occasionally. However, the majority of crises in most jobs are either reoccurring events or crises brought on by something you either did or did not do. When you waste time, you are probably setting up a future crisis. When you put off something you really don't want to do, you almost guarantee that it will turn into a crisis.

EXHIBIT 6–3. Planning a Meeting Worksheet

1. *Objective:*   What end result do you want to achieve?

   _____

   _____

   _____

   _____

2. *Timing:*   How long should the meeting last and when is the best time to hold it? Consider both the day and the time during the day.

   _____

   _____

   _____

   _____

3. *Participants:*   Who should attend? Be sure to include, as appropriate, those with authority to decide, information to be used, whose commitment is needed, or who need to know.

   _____

   _____

   _____

   _____

   _____

4. *Agenda:*   What items should be dealt with? Who is responsible for preparing and distributing the agenda? How will participants be included in developing the agenda?

   _____

   _____

   _____

   _____

   _____

EXHIBIT 6–3. *Continued*

5. *Physical Arrangements:* What facilities and equipment are required? How should the meeting room be arranged?

_____

_____

_____

_____

_____

_____

_____

6. *Role Assignments:* What role assignments need to be made? For example, scribe, secretary, timekeeper, and discussion moderator.

_____

_____

_____

_____

_____

_____

_____

7. *Evaluation Method:* How will the meeting be evaluated in order to improve the next session?

_____

_____

_____

_____

_____

_____

_____

The starting point to reduce the number of crises you experience is to reflect on a significant time period. What crises occurred? Are there any patterns that you can detect? In most situations you can develop responses to recurring events based on historical data. For example, if several crises were experienced due to the breakdown of a particular piece of machinery, how can you either avoid or be prepared to respond to the next breakdown? Can you replace it, have a standby available, or have replacement parts on hand?

Another area for attention was covered in the prior section on contingency planning. Look at the key dimensions of effectiveness on your project such as quality, quantity, cost, and timeliness and think through three questions beforehand so you are ready to respond when the crisis occurs:

- What is likely to go wrong?
- When will I know about it?
- What will I do about it?

Some crises are caused by things that are not within your control. You may have unrealistic deadlines laid on you, priorities may be changed at the last minute, people will make mistakes, machines will break down, there will be delays. When these sorts of things happen, sit back, take a deep breath, and relax for a few minutes. Then think through what has to be done and consider your alternatives. Finally, approach the situation in an orderly, methodical way. You don't want to precipitate a second crisis while trying to handle the first one.

Summary and Conclusions

Time is wasted when it is spent on lower-priority activities. An activity per se is not a time waster. The relevant questions are always: What else might I be doing? and, What is its priority?

There are many potential interferences that might cause you to abandon a high-priority task in favor of a lower-priority one. Some of these come from the environment within which you work; others come from inside yourself. Most can be dealt with by first identifying the ones that apply to you and then pursuing the suggestions offered.

People who approach their work and their life in an organized, methodical way typically get a lot done. Others may be busier, but they accomplish less because much of their time and effort is wasted looking for things, scurrying around in response to new demands, and starting over again and again.

You can reduce, or eliminate, the time wasters in your life. Start by getting organized. Then set priorities and learn to say no to low-priority demands that cause you to become overloaded. Trade off lower-priority commitments for high-priority ones that come up unexpectedly.

Provide time in your schedule for the unexpected. You cannot anticipate everything that will come up. So leave some time each day to handle the crises. Use your own experience as a basis for estimating the number and types of crises to expect. Then develop some contingency plans for handling them. This is the first step in getting off the merry-go-round and changing from a reaction mode of operation to a planning mode.

EXERCISE 6–2.   Procrastination List

Instructions: List all of the things you have been putting off. Include both work and home items. Then, make a commitment to deal with each item. Record an appropriate starting and finishing time for each one.

Item	Start	Finish

EXERCISE 6–3.   Interruption Analysis

Instructions: If interruptions are a problem for you, keep a copy of this worksheet on your desk and record your interruptions for two or three days. Go over your data, see what patterns exist, and do whatever is called for to reduce the frequency and duration of interruptions in the future.

Type		Time			Who Interrupted You?	Nature or Purpose of Interruption
Tel.	Visit	Beg.	End	Total		

IN RETROSPECT

Look back over the ideas in this section and think about them in the context of your present job and work environment.

1. From the list of time wasters you developed, select the three worst ones for you. What are they? How much time a day do they consume? What causes them?

   1. _____

   _____

   _____

   _____

   _____

   2. _____

   _____

   _____

   _____

   _____

   3. _____

   _____

   _____

   _____

   _____

2. What are some possible ways of reducing the impact of these time wasters on you and the use of your time?

   _____

   _____

   _____

   _____

   _____

   _____

   _____

3. Reflect on the ideas presented in the text. What can you use? What ideas do you see making a contribution to the way you manage your area of responsibility?

_____

_____

_____

_____

_____

_____

_____

_____

Personal Needs that Get in the Way of Effective Time Utilization

OBJECTIVES

- **Assess your personal needs that tend to interfere with effective time utilization.**
- **Explore the impact of these needs on your use of time.**
- **Consider ways to restrict or redirect the satisfaction of these needs.**

Many self-generated time wasters are the result of efforts to satisfy personal needs. Frequently, people are unaware of this process. It is most uncommon, for example, to hear someone say, "I have a high need for acceptance and therefore will do whatever you ask in order to satisfy that need." Rather, that individual will take on extra work, respond to every request, and feel good when others express their appreciation. In the meantime other, more important work is left undone. To get a cursory look at your needs profile, complete the Self-Assessment Questionnaire, Exercise 7–1.

Needs Profile Analysis

Social Interaction.   Some people have a high need for contact and interaction with others. If you scored 16 or more in this category, you are in the high need range. If you scored 20 or more, the need is sufficiently strong to be a potential problem in your effective use of time.

Many jobs provide an adequate opportunity for satisfying high social needs during the course of the normal work day. Other jobs, however, provide little opportunity. Problems begin to occur when people with high needs occupy jobs with little built-in opportunity to satisfy those needs. When this situation occurs, the needs typically get satisfied in nonproductive ways.

People with unsatisfied high social needs tend to waste not only their own time but also the time of others in close proximity. They tend to be the drop-in visitors with no particular agenda or a very superficial one at best. Having dropped in, they often are difficult to break away from.

If you fall in this category, two ideas are worth some thought. First, respect the time of others. You may choose to waste your own time, but be considerate of others working around you. Ask if people have time to talk or would it be better for you to come back later. Observe your conversational partner. Does he or she seem anxious to do something else? Watch for such things as standing up and moving away, glancing at papers, or in fact even returning to work by writing or making calculations.

EXERCISE 7–1. Self-Assessment Questionnaire

Instructions: Enter a number to the right to indicate the extent to which you agree or disagree with each item. The response scale is: 5—completely agree, 4—tend to agree, 3—uncertain, 2—tend to disagree, and 1—completely disagree.

Rating

1. I could not work in a job that required me to work alone most, or all, of the time. ____

2. What others think of me is extremely important to me. ____

3. I worry about mistakes I have made in my work. ____

4. I would be terribly embarrassed if someone found an error in some of my work. ____

5. I prefer to be a member of a team rather than to work alone. ____

6. I am pleased when others ask me for assistance, and I will do everything I can to comply. ____

7. I am not satisfied until I have done my very best on any given task or assignment. ____

8. I frequently spend a lot of time studying or analyzing possibilities before I take action. ____

9. A friendly social atmosphere is an important part of a good place to work. ____

10. I frequently subordinate my views and desires to those expressed by others. ____

11. The only way to be sure something is done correctly is to do it yourself. ____

12. Rules and regulations are to be understood and strictly followed. ____

13. It is necessary, and appropriate, to take a portion of the work day for friendly conversation. ____

14. I find it difficult to end conversations even when they interfere with my work schedule. ____

15. I often spend a lot of time correcting or redoing work done by others. ____

EXERCISE 7-1. *Continued*

	Rating
16. I prefer a lot of organization and structure in my job.	———
17. I take a great deal of pride in the number of friends I have.	———
18. I often guess at what someone wants rather than be embarrassed by asking for more information.	———
19. People who turn out less-than-perfect-quality work are either careless or lazy.	———
20. I have a need to include the thoughts and wishes of others in decisions I make that might affect them.	———

Scoring

Instructions: Record the point value of each response on the line corresponding to the item number. Add the values in each column and record the total on the line at the bottom of the column.

Social Interaction	Acceptance	Perfection	Risk Avoidance
1. _____	2. _____	3. _____	4. _____
5. _____	6. _____	7. _____	8. _____
9. _____	10. _____	11. _____	12. _____
13. _____	14. _____	15. _____	16. _____
17. _____	18. _____	19. _____	20. _____
Total _____	_____	_____	_____

The second idea you should pursue is to develop a means to have your social needs satisfied in a productive way. Consider alternatives like getting together at lunch, scheduling break times with colleagues in advance, requesting assignment to ad hoc study teams, and getting involved in activities after working hours.

Acceptance.   Some people have a high need to be accepted by others—to be liked. If you scored 16 or more in this category, you are in the high need range. If you scored 20 or more, the need is sufficiently strong to be a potential problem in your effective use of time.

Many work groups provide an adequate opportunity to satisfy high acceptance needs. The self-worth of individual group members is confirmed through normal interaction patterns and feedback channels. Furthermore, group members cooperate and support each other. They do not make unreasonable demands of one another, and they work together to minimize the impact of demands from outside the group. Not everyone is a member of such a group—either because a job is not part of a group or the group behaves differently.

People with unsatisfied high acceptance needs tend to take on too much to do. They often are viewed as "easy" by others, and others, therefore, frequently take advantage of them. Doing what others ask is the price paid for acceptance, confirmation of self-worth, and being liked. It often is a very high price in terms of alternative use of time. Time is wasted when responding to such requests takes you away from higher-priority work.

If you scored high in this category, these ideas might help you gain better control over the use of your time. First, look for ways to provide your own confirmation of worth. You can do this in two ways. As you address a task, determine the significance of the task and the contribution it can make. Then give it your best effort. When you have finished, reflect on and experience the pride of having completed the task and done it well. Be willing to figuratively pat yourself on the back. Do not depend solely on others for your confirmation. As Emerson said, "The reward for doing a job well is the experience of having done it."

Another way to confirm your self-worth, and thereby reduce your dependency on others, is to take inventory of the things you do well. Frequently in life, attention is directed to what is not done well—where improvement is required. By doing this the positive qualities of individuals are ignored and taken for granted. In Exercise 7–2 list all the things you do well. Include both work and nonwork items. Your goal is a large list, so include everything you can think of and don't be too critical.

Now, how do you deal with the many requests that come your way? Basically by using the advice previously given—learn to say no. Or at least learn to say later. When someone asks you to do something, question its priority or importance. Don't let your judgment be overshadowed by the organizational position of the one making the request. Compare the priority of the request to the priority of what you would otherwise be doing and use one of the following responses, as appropriate.

EXERCISE 7–2. Things I Do Well

_____

- I can take care of that, but in order to do so what I'm now doing will be delayed. Is what you're requesting more important?
- I'll be glad to take care of that for you. However, I can't get to it until I finish what I'm now doing. That will be . . .
- I don't have time to handle that, but you might consider . . .
- I don't have time to handle that, but I'd be glad to loan you my files so you could do it.
- I'm sorry, I just don't have the time to take on any new work. I'll be glad to call you when my schedule frees up?

Perfection.   Some people set very high standards for themselves. They have a need to achieve as close to perfection as possible. If you scored 16 or more in this category, you are in the high need range. If you scored 20 or more, the need is sufficiently strong to be a potential problem in your effective use of time.

Some tasks require very high quality output. As such, spending extra time checking and rechecking to ensure nearly perfect performance is justified. However, many of the things that one does do not require that same degree of quality. The key is to be able to distinguish between the ones requiring high quality and those that do not. Then invest your time to achieve near perfect results when required but don't waste time to attain perfection when it is not required.

People who score low in this category, for example less than 10, may also be wasting time. Because of low quality standards, they may end up having to redo work that does not meet minimum standards of acceptability. The investment of a little more time the first time could save substantially later by eliminating the need to start over.

If this area is a problem for you, begin by obtaining a clear understanding of the quality expected by the one assigning you the work. Ask questions: Do you want a precise or an approximate answer? How much time and money are you willing to spend to enhance the quality of the product? What quality level are you looking for? What is the lower cutoff on your range of acceptable quality?

Another thought is also worth considering. Time and effort invested in quality assurance should not exceed the cost of potential error. This notion simply says you need a positive return on your investment. To get there, you must first estimate the cost of potential error. If it is low, you can't afford to spend a lot of time to eliminate all errors. If the cost is high, you obviously should take the time.

The personal costs of perfectionism can be great. When standards are too high, there will be very few times when they are achieved. This will often lead to disappointment due to the infrequent opportunities to experience success. Constant disappointment can have severe negative impact on people's attitudes.

Risk Avoidance.   Some people have a high need to avoid risk. They are unwilling to try the new and unproven, to take unpopular stands on issues, or to test the limits of the world within which they exist. If you scored 16 or more in this category, you are in the high need range. If you scored 20 or more, the need is sufficiently strong to be a potential problem in your effective use of time.

People with a high need to avoid risk typically take more time studying and analyzing options, checking with others to obtain concurrence, and waiting or hesitating to take action. Again, there may be times when any or all of these time-consuming activities are justified. The problem comes from an absence of differentiation based on some valid criterion.

If this area is a problem for you, examine what is at stake in the cases when you find yourself taking *more time than justified* before rendering a decision or taking action. What is at risk? What will happen if it doesn't work out? Will you be embarrassed? Will you get fired? Will someone be seriously injured? Will the company lose a lot of money? Your next line of thought should explore the question: What will happen if it does work out? Will you get what you want? Will you meet the deadline? Will you save the company a lot of money? Will it improve the business? Now, look at the potential payoff and the potential cost of the opportunity you face. Which is more likely to occur? Is the potential payoff worth the risk? If so, move forward with conviction. If not, abandon the idea and don't look back.

There simply is no way to eliminate all risk. It's a normal part of life brought about by an inability to see the future. Foolish action obviously is to be avoided. But calculated risks should be taken when there is a high probability of a positive outcome.

Applying Needs Assessment Results

Take the two categories in which you scored highest and reflect on your experience. Record your observations in response to the questions in Exercise 7–3.

EXHIBIT 7-3. Dealing with Personal Needs

1. The need category in which you scored highest is: _____
   _____

2. How do you generally fulfill this need? Does the fulfillment of this need interfere with your effective use of time? If so, in what ways?
   _____
   _____
   _____
   _____
   _____

3. How can you reduce or eliminate the negative consequences of this need on your effective use of time?
   _____
   _____
   _____
   _____
   _____

4. The need category in which you scored second highest is:_____

5. How do you generally fulfill this need? Does the fulfillment of this need interfere with your effective use of time? If so, in what ways?
   _____
   _____
   _____
   _____
   _____

6. How can you reduce or eliminate the negative consequence of this need on your effective use of time?
   _____
   _____
   _____
   _____
   _____

Summary and Conclusions

Personal needs often get in the way of effective time utilization. Needs for social interaction, acceptance, perfection, and risk avoidance are common examples.

Personal needs have a way of commanding your attention until they are satisfied. To avoid having them interfere with the effective use of your time, either seek alternative means of satisfaction or learn to moderate them. For example, social interaction can take place outside work hours. And, perhaps acceptance, perfection, and risk avoidance can be moderated.

The personal need that creates a time problem for you may not be one of these. However, with some careful self-examination, you should be able to identify your particular cause of concern. Then proceed to get it under control.

IN RETROSPECT

Reflect upon the ideas presented in this section and consider them in the context of your present job and work environment.

1. What have you learned about yourself and your use of time as a result of the information and activities in this section?

   _____

   _____

   _____

   _____

   _____

   _____

2. What opportunities do you see to make better use of your time and also get your needs met?

   _____

   _____

   _____

   _____

   _____

   _____

3. Do others that you deal with waste your time in the process of fulfilling their needs? If so, how might you limit the impact of this on your time?

_____

_____

_____

_____

_____

_____

4. How might you change your work group to provide more productive ways for group members to satisfy their personal needs?

_____

_____

_____

_____

_____

_____

5. What other ideas have you gained from this section that can help you improve upon your time utilization?

_____

_____

_____

_____

_____

_____

Section 8.

Planning for Improvement

OBJECTIVES

- **Apply the study guide to your job and work situation.**
- **Develop specific plans to use the concepts and techniques studied.**
- **Motivate you to initiate action to improve your use of time.**

How much influence can you exert over your use of time? Probably a lot more than you realize. The opportunity is there if you choose to take advantage of it.

Some people react negatively to the idea of action planning. They are of the opinion that they will use whatever ideas they find useful whether or not they develop specific plans to do so. Experience suggests that this is unlikely. All of the good intentions are quickly lost, and those without plans change few if any of the ways they use their time. Remember: Objectives with plans are both directive and energizing. They not only point the way but motivate you to initiate change. Don't lose the value of this very positive force.

You have been exposed to a number of ideas that can be used to improve your time utilization. In this section you will examine your own use of time and develop an action plan for improvement. During the process, consider all of the ideas you developed as you worked through each section. If you have responded to the exercises to this point, your action planning will essentially be a consolidating and prioritizing of what you have already written.

This action planning activity is divided into three parts. First is stating your objective. That is what you want to accomplish. Next is listing opportunities. This step basically looks at ways to accomplish your objective. Then comes the actual action planning. At this point you look at the steps required to achieve your objective, the sequence in which they occur, and the target date for completion.

When you complete this section, you will have a detailed road map showing you how to better use your time. Good luck!

---

1. List your weekly objectives and prioritize them

2. Make a daily "To Do" list and prioritize it

3. Always start with the A's

4. Handle each piece of paper only once

5. Ask, "What is the best use of my time right now?"

6. Don't procrastinate—do it now!

FIGURE 8–1. Six tips for effective time management

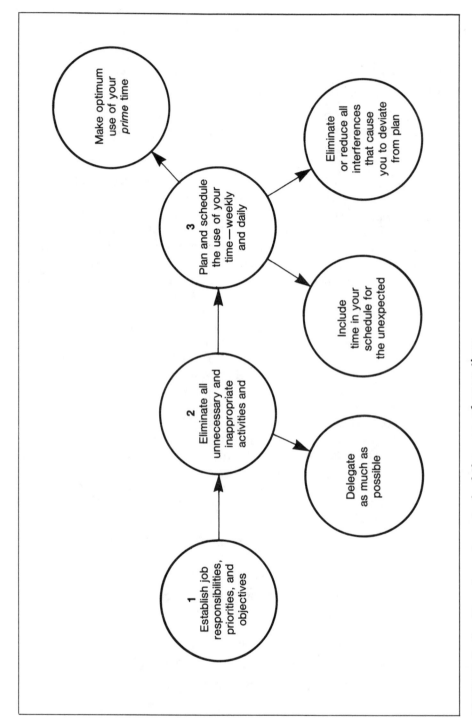

FIGURE 8–2. How to get control of the use of your time

EXERCISE 8–1. Planning for Improved Time Utilization

What is your objective? Be specific both in terms of how much time you hope to free up in your weekly schedule and the target date by which you hope to accomplish it.

_____

_____

_____

What areas of opportunity exist for you? Again, be specific. What tasks might be eliminated or reassigned? What time wasters can be eliminated or reduced? What planning needs to be done?

Opportunity	Estimated Time Savings
_____	_____
_____	_____
_____	_____
_____	_____
_____	_____
_____	_____
_____	_____
_____	_____
_____	_____
_____	_____
_____	_____
_____	_____
_____	_____
_____	_____
_____	_____
_____	_____
_____	_____
_____	_____
_____	_____

EXERCISE 8–1. *Continued*

Select out of your list of opportunities those that you would like to pursue and when accomplished would add up to your targeted time savings. (Space is provided for planning to accomplish three. If you want to address more, please use the backs of pages or additional sheets of paper.)

Opportunity No. 1: _____

_____

_____

Action Steps	Target Dates

EXERCISE 8–1. *Continued*

Opportunity No. 2: _____

_____

_____

Action Steps	*Target Dates*
_____	_____
_____	_____
_____	_____
_____	_____
_____	_____
_____	_____
_____	_____
_____	_____
_____	_____
_____	_____

Opportunity No. 3: _____

_____

_____

Action Steps	*Target Dates*
_____	_____
_____	_____
_____	_____
_____	_____
_____	_____
_____	_____
_____	_____
_____	_____
_____	_____

EXERCISE 8–1. *Continued*

Who needs to be involved and to what extent in carrying out this change effort? This would include review and approval of plans as well as cooperating with you and taking on certain duties and responsibilities.

Supervisor: _____

_____

_____

_____

_____

_____

_____

Associates: _____

_____

_____

_____

_____

_____

_____

Staff: _____

_____

_____

_____

_____

_____

_____

Follow Up—Staying on Track

OBJECTIVES

- **Monitor your progress in making better use of your time.**
- **Hold your interest in pursuing your time management objectives.**
- **Demonstrate the gains that can be made when plans are implemented.**
- **Establish new time management habits.**

Now that you've finished this study, what next? Will you leave all your good intentions and continue the same old habits you've always had? Or will you follow through on the plans developed and really begin to get control of your time? The choice is up to you.

As originally acknowledged, no one has complete control over his or her time. However, you do control a portion of it. And even when you do not have control over what you do, you always have some degree of freedom in how you do it. Thus, we have the two basic approaches to better time utilization. First, develop the greatest degree of efficiency in handling those things that must be done. Don't put them off. Get organized. Systematize the routine as much as you can. Second, in the time remaining, address your highest priority demands. Develop good personal work habits to cut down on wasted time. Learn to say no to work that overloads you or trade it for lower-priority work already assigned.

It's reported that anyone can change any habit in two weeks. All that's required is that the motivation be sufficient to make it worth your while. This follow-up section allows you to monitor your progress for six weeks. Within that period not only can you change habits but you can get the new behavior patterns well ingrained. Monitor your progress and record your results on the progress report and the progress chart. At the end of six weeks, complete the progress survey. By then, tremendous improvement should be clearly evident.

EXERCISE 9–1. Time Savings Progress Report

Instructions: Record the progress you make each week in your efforts to better manage your time. What unnecessary or inappropriate tasks did you eliminate? What use did you make of planning? How has it helped? What time wasters were you able to eliminate or reduce?

First week: _____

_____

_____

_____

_____

_____

_____

_____

Second week: _____

_____

_____

_____

_____

_____

_____

_____

Third week: _____

_____

_____

_____

_____

_____

_____

_____

EXERCISE 9–1. *Continued*

Fourth week: _____

_____

_____

_____

_____

_____

_____

_____

Fifth week: _____

_____

_____

_____

_____

_____

_____

Sixth week: _____

_____

_____

_____

_____

_____

_____

_____

EXERCISE 9–2.   Time Savings Progress Chart

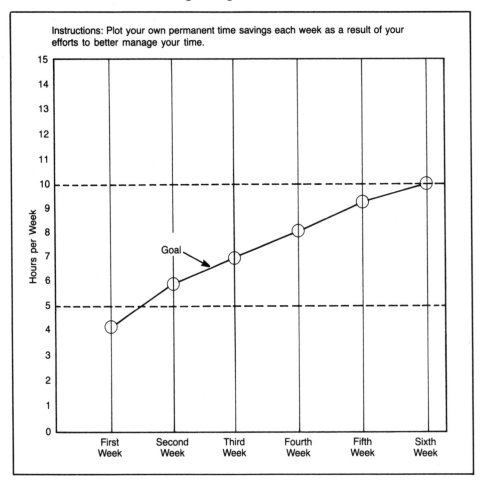

Instructions: Plot your own permanent time savings each week as a result of your efforts to better manage your time.

EXERCISE 9–3.   Time Management Progress Survey

Instructions: Six weeks after working through this text, complete this summary of your progress. It will show you where you are doing well and where you still need to devote some attention.

Scoring key: Yes = 1, Usually = 2, Sometimes = 3, Rarely = 4, Never or No = 5, Not Applicable = NA

1. Do you have a clearly defined list of written objectives?   ———

2. Do you plan and schedule your time on a weekly and daily basis?   ———

3. Can you find large blocks of uninterrupted time when you need to?   ———

4. Have you eliminated frequently recurring crises from your job?   ———

5. Do you refuse to answer the phone when engaged in important conversations?   ———

6. Do you use travel and waiting time productively?   ———

7. Do you delegate as much as you can?   ———

8. Do you prevent your staff from delegating their tasks and decision making to you?   ———

9. Do you take time each day to think about what you are doing and trying to accomplish?   ———

10. Have you eliminated any time wasters during the past week?   ———

11. Do you feel really in control of your time?   ———

12. Is your desk and office well organized and free of clutter?   ———

13. Have you eliminated time wasted in meetings?   ———

14. Have you conquered your tendency to procrastinate?   ———

EXERCISE 9–3. *Continued*

15. Do you carry out your work on the basis of priorities? _____

16. Do you resist the temptation to get overly involved in your staff's activities? _____

17. Do you control your schedule so that others do not waste time waiting for you? _____

18. Do you meet your deadlines? _____

19. Can you identify the critical few tasks that account for the majority of your results? _____

20. Are you better organized and accomplishing more than you were six weeks ago? _____

21. Have you been able to reduce the amount of time you spend on routine paperwork? _____

22. Do you effectively control interruptions and drop-in visitors? _____

23. Have you mastered the ability to say no whenever you should? _____

24. Do you spend enough time training your staff? _____

25. Have you stopped taking work home? _____

26. Do you stay current with all your reading? _____

27. Do you have enough time for yourself—recreation, study, community service, family? _____

TOTAL   _____

Scoring: Add the points assigned to each item. The lower your score, the better. Look particularly at those items you rated 4 or 5. These represent challenges for further development.

_____

From *The Time Management Workbook*, Merrill E. Douglas, Time Management Center, Grandville, MI, p. 16, © 1982. Used by permission of the author. All rights reserved.

About the Author

Marion E. Haynes is an adult educator specializing in supervisory and management training. He began his career in employee relations with a major oil company in California in 1956. He was in charge of a division employee relations function with a staff of five when he was selected for a head office assignment. Following a year as a labor relations advisor, he moved to management and organization development in 1968. Since then he has specialized in the design, presentation, and evaluation of management training.

As a professional educator, Haynes's horizons extend beyond his primary employer through public speaking, writing, and service. He presents a series of management training workshops under the sponsorship of several universities in the south-central states. He also has been an invited speaker at several trade and professional association gatherings. He currently serves as a member of the advisory panel to Texas A&M's management training division and the advisory board of Houston Baptist University's professional development division. He has published more than twenty articles in both professional and trade journals and two previous books—*Stepping Up to Supervisor* (PennWell 1983) and *Managing Performance* (Lifetime Learning Publications 1984).

Haynes was awarded the BS degree in business administration with a minor in psychology by Arizona State University in 1956. He also holds the MBA with distinction in management from New York University. He is currently listed in the *Directory of Distinguished Americans* and *Personalities of the South*.